# Bamako Boom Boom

Misha Somerville in West Africa

Published in 2009 by Stingray Publications
ISBN 978-0-9561730-0-3

all written content copyright © Misha Somerville 2008
all photos copyright as credited:
Copyright © Misha Somerville 2007
Copyright © Damien Dussut 2007
Copyright © Peter Clausen 2007

Cover Design & Illustration
Somhairle MacDonald @ Schmo - www.schmo.biz
Copyright © Somhairle MacDonald 2009

Printed by the MPG Books Group in the UK

'to travel till your eyes can open no further'

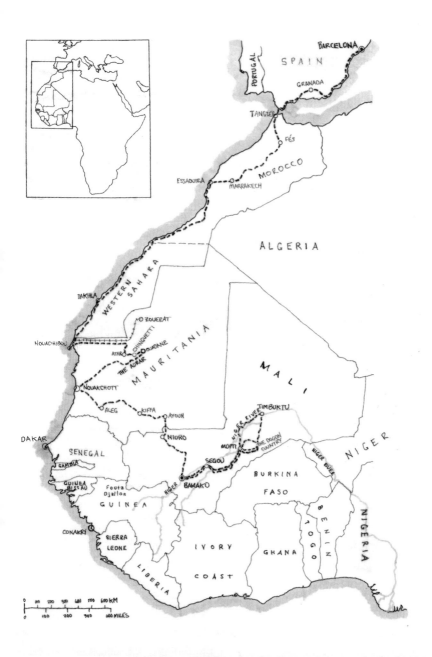

# Stepping Out

There should always be a time for shutting the eyes, jumping in and worrying about the consequences later. Thank god we weren't wearing any clothes, or I'd have been scrubbing harbour sludge out of them for months.

A Saturday in December was a night out with friends and colleagues in Barcelona. For some reason it had seemed like a good idea to jump off the harbour at 4am, failing to board a moored wooden yacht in the process, and probably for the best really. But the swim had woken me up and by the time we were back at the hotel I was on a roll and I felt like it was time to go. If I was to stay, it would be a case of extricating myself with a hangover from a Barcelona Hotel room the following day - I might even change my mind and go back to Scotland with everyone else. It was time to make the break and with best wishes from all I ran down the hotel stairs and out the door: destination Dakar, Senegal.

In my haste however, I hadn't checked the bus timetable, so with a four hour wait I ended up sleeping in the bus station, trying to grab forty winks while playing cat and mouse with the station master who moved me on every twenty minutes. Despite a regular alarm clock, in the form of the pissed off Spaniard, I still almost missed the bus.

It was by coincidence that a friend of mine, Sam, planned to be staying in a cave in Granada, in the south of Spain. Finding someone in a cave in a city sounded like a long shot, but I thought I'd give it a bash anyway.

The bus picked it's way down the Coast of Spain, my hangover quite fittingly in full swing as I opened my eyes and Benidorm passed by the window. It was 4am when the bus rolled into Granada, setting me out to another cold night in a bus station.  At this point at least it seemed unwise not to have taken a jacket.

The sun came up and the hunt for the cave was on.  I asked around but not knowing the Spanish for 'cave' proved awkward. Even drawing a cave seemed difficult - it only became a cave when you drew a fire outside it for some reason.  Eventually an old man cottoned on to what I was looking for – older people seem to have more patience with language difficulties - waving his arm in a vague direction.  Following his arm, I walked up a hill, by the famous Alhambra, a palace where the walls are ornamented with such complex patterns that in modern terms they scarcely believe it possible to construct a building such as this, a fact which had almost earned it a place as one of the Seven Wonders of the Modern World.  I'd have to say it was a little complicated for my taste - although impressive.  I continued on and as the city opened out beneath, the much more basic caves came into sight.  First there was one, then two, and then a whole hillside.  Which one would Sam be in?  There was only one way to find out - to ask around - and had it not been for my ensuing goose chase, I would never so quickly have worked out what the caves were all about.

There are about three hundred caves that sit above Granada looking out over the city.  The people who live in them, from all over Europe if not the world, are poets, sculptors, musicians, talkers, thinkers and more - probably amongst the most rag tag group of people I've met.  They live for free, recycling stuff from the streets, and earning a few extra Euros for alcohol or olives, amongst other things, from hair brained money making schemes.  You don't have to pay any rent for any of the caves, at least not in this part of the world, and you could probably find an empty one if you just turned up, although you might have to be a little more patient for one of the better ones.

I arrived at lunchtime, when only a few people were milling about. I met a Pole and an Australian who talked about the improvements they have been making to their caves. The Pole only works at night, under candle light, making an incredible, intricate wall in his cave – way more elaborate than to serve any functional purpose. The Australian was just keeping to the basics, and fitting a door.

As it turned out that day, most people had gone to a rave on the other side of the city at 11am – it seemed like an odd time for a rave but I didn't ask too many questions. I met an Irish Guy, Oisín, who was wandering about with some whisky in order to get those left behind out of their beds. On account of Sam's Irishness I fancied Oisín might lead me to the man I was looking for, so I wandered round with him, helping out with the round, which is carried out like some sort of daily public service - the postal service, only it's whisky not letters.

This is the 'crazy' Branca [cave community] and as I found out through the day there are five in total, including two Gipsy Brancas and one less chaotic one. Unsuccessful with my hunt in the first one, I moved on.

In the second, more peaceful, Branca, the ingenious ways the caves had been developed showed that these residents had been living there for much longer. The caves in this Branca sat into the terraced hillside, with small gardens and patios outside, where you could sit and look out over the city and pontificate. Inside, it seemed that if you wanted an extra shelf or another room, you just dug it out. The caves sometimes went as far as having painted walls with pictures hanging from them, bedrooms and kitchens with electricity. If you had a DVD player people would come from all over the hillside to watch a film. I thought it was strange that this should all seem so amazing, after all, most houses would have had all this and more, but the fact they were caves somehow added an extra charm.

It was while knocking on doors that I realised how multinational the occupants were. You weren't sure how to start the conversation, what response you might get, how you might start communicating or where it might take you, but that was the thrill of it. I doubt you would find such a cosmopolitan community even in New York, where nationalities are segregated into neighbourhoods.

I continued to trail about on the path to try and find Sam, joining the dots in a zig zag fashion from cave to cave. For several hours I followed people's directions but then realised this Sam, the one I was being directed to, bore no resemblance to my friend.

I ended up drinking tea in a cave with a Polish/Czech couple – Roman and Ivona – whose cave I'd knocked on the door of. We chatted for hours, emptying the tea pot several times as I learned about living in the caves. I asked about the big building at the top of the hill – a delinquents school I had passed earlier where the children were playing football with the Gypsies. Roman mentioned a girl had her arm broken when some Gypsies chased her out of her cave just recently. He also mentioned that the City Council had planned to fill the caves in with concrete. They certainly wouldn't be the Council's favourite neighbourhood as I couldn't see them having much success collecting any kind of Council Tax from the caves. It seemed that the constant threat of being evicted was part of living here. The community had survived as an almost unique haven in Western Europe - one which propagated a lifestyle which captured people's imaginations. Vague rumours of its existence, spread by word-of-mouth through Europe, North Africa and beyond, helped it attain a near mythical status and drew people in to visit or to live. I left Roman and Ivona's with a promise of a place to stay for the night should I need it.

It seemed like a hopeless mission - I gave up on finding Sam and walked back into the city. He had been walking across the Pyrenees for several months, and a vague email sent a week previously was not enough to convince me he was in Granada at all. But back in the city I was sitting in an internet café when he popped up in my inbox, and an hour later I met him under the Alhambra. I laughed – I could have just let technology do the hard part in the first place, but where's the fun in that?

We spent the next few days living in the caves – Michel (Israel), Acha (dog), Anna (Sweden) and Walter, a Canadian writer with a curiosity for everything. Others came and went, Sergio arrived with Chai, sweet bread and songs. The view that stretched out, looking down from the door of our cave to the glistening lights of the city in the valley, reminded me of something too big to comprehend….but strangely many things seem to make sense here.
[Note from Anna:]

*Misha: Thank you for living in the cueva [cave] with us for a while. I am sure Africa will give you everything you need and more. I want to go there so much! Later, mañana mañana, whenever you want- come to Sweden! Just write or phone, and do it if you don't come also, if you feel like it. Maybe one night under the stars in Africa, in the desert, in a phone booth, maybe you feel you need to speak with a Swedish person. Take care.*

*Much Love, Anna*

# Meeting The Salesmen

Africa welcomes you at Tangier with the world's best touts and shysters. I've heard this described as the most unwelcoming entrance to any continent in the world. For centuries this port has been the jugular vein in Afro-European trade, so I guess it's only natural that the people here have become experts in creaming off anything they can rather than making anything of their own. The situation has improved in the last decade as the Moroccan government, keen to boost tourism, has clamped down on the harassment of visitors to the country, introducing a specific tourist police force to change the lawless perception of the country's primary overland entry point. It seemed if you weren't too affected by the perception of lawlessness, it would be a pretty exciting town.

I walked down the narrow alleys of the market where the scooters, animals, bicycles and children ran. The cafes spilled out on to the streets; packed out and sometimes two or three storeys high, a mass of vociferously animated and larger-than-life Moroccans, gambling; playing cards, dominos and board games in an atmosphere turbo charged by a constant stream of coffee and cigarettes. This is a hustlers town, seductive and menacing for a white European with a rucksack, whose presence is noticed by all.

I forgot the time, and in a rush to get the bus on to Fès, I took a wrong turn, ending up in a dimly lit corner of the castle overlooking the bay and passing a shady looking group of guys who fell silent when they saw me. They know I'm coming to a dead end, but I don't yet. In an effort to not look like a gormless tourist, an easy target, I pretend to go for a piss, turning back and trying to look as confident as possible walking by them and on to find the bus.

It seemed that African buses always let you out at the time you least want it, like in Fès at 3am. I'm sure finding a place to stay would not have been so difficult had I known the city, but as it was, I ended up traipsing about, going round in circles trying to work out what was what, what was where and where was what. A city, when it's unfamiliar, is just a giant maze. A few hours later, after banging on doors and more doors, I got a bed in an expensive hotel but moved on to a hostel in the morning on account of cost - the plan being to hang around in Fès for a few days as it sounded like an interesting place. It is considered to be the cultural capital of Morocco, and usually the starting point for political unrest, where for whatever reason, people take to the streets in protest more readily than elsewhere in Morocco.

In the sunshine of the following day I met an older chap in a café, Abdul, who told me about the city guides and how they work on commission. So you hire a guide for a fixed price – I paid 100Dh (about 10 Euro). Fair enough. You pay for all the taxis, coffees, etc - also fair enough, I would say. But a leisurely taxi tour of the city soon turns into an intense join-the-dots trip round shops and boutiques. You're accosted by the salesmen at each until you want nothing more than for them to get out of your face, even if that means giving them money for some inane piece of tat you never wanted. It works for them – a well travelled friend of mine once said that the Moroccans were the best in the world when it comes to getting money out of you. Despite my repetitively reinforced excuse that I was travelling across Africa with an over-the-shoulder bag and had nowhere to put carpets, silverware, pots, leather bags, shawls, jumpers, jackets, sculptures, etc etc, I still came away with a hat (that was too small for me) and a bag (that fell apart 2 weeks later in the desert). But the shopkeepers love the American tourists - shipping oversize packages of Moroccan goods by cargo back to their homeland. The guides get a commission from the shopkeepers for having taken the Westerners to them to be accosted. My guide (also called Abdul) gets pissed off – I'm a bad customer so his commission from the afternoon will be small.  He eventually mellows out when we get a coffee in the middle of the maze,  I start asking him about his life and family, and he realises that I'm actually interested in Morocco and not just being awkward.  He almost looks surprised; in Africa where the West is often seen as the land of freedom and plenty, the idea that Westerners are interested in anything more than buying stuff comes as a shock.  He's also surprised by the fact that I would choose to travel to Dakar on my own.

Because previous generations of Europeans visiting Morocco (and Africa in general) splashed their money about like kings, the Moroccans see it as their continuing mission to get a slice of yours. It's fair enough really, but as you go about your life you have no idea  who to trust, and so you waste time and energy constantly checking you are getting a fair price for things, that your pockets are closed and your camera is out of sight.  It's a pain to constantly have to think about holding on to your money, about not being ripped off or robbed.  In Scotland I rarely need to think about money, most people would sooner buy you a pint than steal your wallet. In Africa, nothing has a fixed price; it depends on who you are, and if you are a westerner then you are presumed, and probably quite rightly, to be comparatively rich.  I don't actually mind paying a little more than the locals for things, but the culture of trying to cheat you I find difficult.  In other poor parts of the world I've been to, I've found that people get more welcoming and generous the poorer they are.  It's perhaps because you are more likely to invite a stranger into your house to stay if you have nothing in your house worth stealing, or maybe even just because poor people are more used to sharing things.

Even so, Fès' old town is an awesome experience. In Moroccan towns and cities the old town usually takes the form of a 'Medina'. Sometimes there can be more than one in a town. It's almost like a compact mud city - thousands of narrow alley-ways, tightly packed and going in various directions within the main medina walls, like some sort of insect colony.   Town planning isn't a priority, but somehow it seems to work.  Stalls, boutiques and workshops line the alleyways which form a through-route for carts, goats, cats, mopeds, mules, bikes, chicken and of course people. For a westerner, at least those who look like they are new to the Medina (and it's very difficult not to as hard as I tried), the situation is intensified by the fact that every man-and-his-dog is trying to get your attention to lure you into their shop…every-man-and-his-dog that is, apart from the pick-pockets who, of course, are working by stealth. I had my usual skater-style chains attaching keys and wallet to my belt and spotted the kids eyeing up their chances of pinching them. None went for it.  I even had a laugh with a few after they realised that they were watching my wallet…and I was watching them, watching my wallet. The Moroccans are never afraid to laugh and keeping your sense of humour gets you out of all sorts of sticky corners - some of which you maybe shouldn't have been in in the first place but, like Jack and the Beanstalk, you couldn't help yourself.

Eventually the Medina wears you down. The intensity turns your brain numb.  Everywhere you look is mayhem: carcasses, rotting meat and swarming flys, shouting salesmen, children crying, laughing or shouting, wiry cats crawl about in the shadows, spices coloured to cure the blind sit out in baskets, chickens hang tied and waiting for their time and fish that have had theirs lie in piles. The sweat and dirt oozes over your skin. I sat on a step and watched a kid spitting at the fish sitting out on a stall across the alleyway.

# Family Man

Abdul's tip off about the guide's in Fès had been right. When I met him the next day he pushed it one stage further. 'Don't trust anyone in Morocco, only trust me' he said, his false teeth moving about with a life of their own, completely out of sync with his jaws like in some sort of badly over-dubbed film. It's a strange statement to make, usually having the opposite effect on me to that intended. But on this occasion, after my Medina experience, I was prepared to almost agree with him.

He seemed decent enough, so when he offered me a tour of the city in his car I went along. We talked on the way round, he had pretty good English, saying he worked for the French consulate, although he seemed old enough to be retired which was possibly why he had time to show me about. He invited me to his house for some 'real Moroccan food', promptly phoning his wife to get the meal on. Abdul was a wealthy man by Moroccan standards. His wife, his second, was a full thirty years younger than him and from a big family in the Atlas Mountains in the South of Morocco. He had a daughter studying in France by his previous wife who had died some years ago, and a three year old son with his current wife. They seemed like really decent folk but I could tell their marriage wasn't made for the right reasons. Arguments would start any time I was not in the room, although it was difficult to tell if they were shouting at their child, or each other. His wife did all the housework and both seemed used to, even if not comfortable with, the fact that she was there to serve him. He provided the money.

Abdul likes a drink and a smoke, a privilege which seemed reserved for men, so while we sat, his wife ran around us. Trying to help only suggested that she wasn't doing her job properly, made things worse.  Nonetheless I enjoyed talking to them.   After some beers, spirits and a smoke of some Moroccan he drove me back to the hostel, the drink driving policy being more lax here.

On the way James Brown's ' I feel good' came on the radio and for a few minutes we were cruising through Fès' old town with the windows down, singing and head banging with the car stereo pumping out 'I feel good, da na na na na naa, I knew that I would da na na na na naa … now I feel good, I knew that I would, now... So good......so good, I got you Whoa!...' Funnily enough Abdul was about the sanest man I met in Morocco.  Even so, he still tried to sell me some jewellery and a Berber cloak before I left for Marrakech, saying 'take this, you will need it for the desert cold'. Looking back he may have had a point, but I had no space in my bag, so feeling obliged I just got something small.

# Finding the People

As a sign of things to come further into Africa, we got a puncture on the night bus on the way to Marrakech. When we finally arrived, it took an hour of negotiating to get somewhere to stay before I put my head down for a few hours sleep. Marrakech is Morocco's tourist centre, and it was just filling up with European Christmas-breakers looking for a short break in the sun. I quickly got bored with the market - it's all about the money - and then wondered how can you be bored in a city like this? My boredom didn't last for long. I took my brave pills, hired a moped and boosted out to one of the shanty towns on the outskirts of the city. My heart beat faster the further out of town I got. I had tried to get a beaten up old scooter but the new-style Honda I had made me stick out like a sore thumb. I wrapped my camera in my neck scarf as I passed an army base.

The houses got gradually lower as I drove, until on the edge of the city, and just before the desert took over, they were just mud huts. The first time I went through the slum I didn't stop driving till I reached the rubbish strewn football pitch the edge of the city. Mopeds are not the best for stealth in an unmotorised shanty town. Everyone looked out at me from deep-set eyes and with stern expressions and groups of kids shouted in my direction. For one second, a girl going into one of the mud houses waved at me; maybe it was all the rubbish and turmoil that surrounded her, the excitement of the situation or just her beauty that made it such a strong image, one that remains near crystal clear in my memory.

I was pre-programmed to keep going, trying to look confident and like I knew where I was going, but in a maze of unorganised alleyways with dead ends everywhere, it's difficult. I had no reason to believe that I'd get into trouble, other than the fact that the possessions I had with me probably amounted to several years' work for any of the people living here - but I had seen no evidence to suggest they were violent.  One of the things about travelling alone is that you have to rely on your own judgement completely, making it more exciting.

I took another road out of town in a different direction, but it was as dull as a Saturday night in Tescos - suburban Marrakech.  It wasn't long before I was back in the shanty town.  It's amazing the difference it makes if you've been somewhere before; I smiled at some people, realising that I hadn't on my previous trip through the shanty town, and got amazing smiles back...from everyone.  I don't think I smiled at a single person in Africa without getting a smile back.

This time I rode into the centre of the shanty town, pulled up and turned the motor off.  Some older ladies found my presence there amusing.  Perhaps unsurprisingly everyone noticed me, and some teenagers came over to speak.  They started in French and Spanish and despite the minute amount I understood, I could see our similarities in attitude and humour.  I really missed a language to speak to them in.  Here I was in a Moroccan shanty town, with the chance of an interesting insight into what their life might be like, possibly even spending Christmas there, but what made it difficult was the fact I couldn't talk to them.  We still tried of course.  Six languages; Spanish, French, English, Arabic, Mandarin and some Slavic, maybe Russian - would have most of the world covered.  It can't be that difficult can it?  Well.

I asked to take a photo of the ladies and, feeling slightly guilty, offered them a little money, although some food would have been better.  Refreshingly, they declined on both accounts, not like people in tourist town.

The neighbourhood was lively. It was clearly a bit of a surprise I was there, and all the people who walked by had something to say; possibly a joke at my expense for all I knew, but we had a great time anyway. Eventually I turned back after one last run through the shanty town.

Later on, while walking around the Medina, I got lost and stumbled into the manufacturing quarter of Marrakech. Like in the shanty town, the absence of salesmen came as a breath of fresh air, but they were replaced with a different kind of frenzied chaos. It's nine in the evening on the week before Christmas and the workshops of Marrakech are working over-time. It's like stepping back in time. The night darkness adds to the atmosphere which has an air of Dickensian London about it. Everything moves by donkey and cart through these narrow alleyways. Here the streets are quiet and dirty, piled with wooden barrels and scrap. Peering through gaps in the shoddily built walls, I can see the welders' flash reflecting off the walls and illuminating the heads of scores of dirty children banging, shaping and painting. It's difficult to know whether to see this as exploitative child labour or the production of skillfully made Moroccan craft - the continuation of a tradition. In any case the market where they are sold is only half a mile away, whereas our Loch Ness Monster souvenirs are often made in China (and end up in Japan amongst other places).

The discovery of this dark corner of Marrakech had sucked my mind into a time warp, until, tripping along, I finally snapped out of it. I was lost, and paid some street kids to show me the way back to the main square.

Shanty towns and sweat shops, tourist boutiques and grand guest houses, Marrakech is a colourful place.

# Falling Out With the Gatekeeper

A hop, a skip and a bus ride from Marrakech is the coastal town of Essaouira, a place which stands apart from the rest of Morocco. With it's maverick surfer population Essaouira has a Californian laid back charm to it. It came to reputation in the 60's as the hangout of Jimi Hendrix and Pink Floyd and has since been popularised by French Ex-pats and Artisans. It seemed like a cool place to spend Christmas.

On a sunny Christmas Eve, I'm shuffling round Essaouira's cafés trying to find somewhere to stay. Three touts followed me from the bus station trying to steer me to one of their 'friends' hotels so they could collect their commission. I ran out of languages to say 'fuck off' in. I'd had enough of single rooms in hotels – it's no craic staying by yourself. When you've only got a few days in a place you've not got long to work out what it's all about. While expensive hotels might be good if you want your full eight hours, there's nothing like being wedged in some skanky hostel in a dodgy part of town to get your finger firmly on the pulse. I went for a policy of asking who-ever looked cool if they knew somewhere good to stay. As it was, the very first person who I asked, a dreadlocked guy called Hisham, not only knew a little English from some time spent in Europe (pretty unusual for a Moroccan) but also had a room in his apartment. Just half an hour later we were round the table drinking beer and listening to psy-trance. The flat turned out to be the meeting place for Hisham's circle of friends and anyone else that they managed to pick up on the streets (like me). Among them were a couple of Dutch surfers who had been coming to the Moroccan coast for years. Very unfortunately they had been attacked by machete wielding bandits while camping out to the South of

Essaouira on their last trip. Luckily they got away with some missing equipment and a few slashes to the arms which a private clinic in Morocco stitched up, but the whole experience obviously hadn't been enough to dissuade them from coming back...the waves must be good around here.

We all drank some beer, then some vodka, and then some other local spirit - I've got no idea what it was. Hisham and his brother were so stoned that they collapsed into bed not to be seen till the following evening. Myself and another guy, Amin, went out to drink some more, sit on the beach wall, chat and play some music. Amin is one of these guys that gives you the impression he's carrying around his life's possessions on his back. He's got an uncased guitar which he plays on occasion, usually to give a brilliant rendition of Pink Floyd's 'Wish You Were Here'. In the few days I know him for he sings it at least a dozen times – it must be difficult when you are so good at singing such a brilliant song that anything else is just a disappointment. We wandered about like a couple of stray cats, happily floating with no objective. I find few things so positively life affirming as becoming instant friends with someone from a completely different culture and place. In many cases you might never see or hear from that person again, but that only seems to make the time more memorable.

Later on, a racist disagreement at a party between Amin, of Berber origin, and the host of the party, an Arab, makes it best for us to leave before getting ourselves in any more trouble. We drank till the small hours in a small music club, before realising we hadn't eaten in a long time. A bit of local knowledge helped out with knowing where to go and we managed to get some sort of burger from a bunch of people hanging out round a fire on a street corner, I'd have had them down as neds but I was finding it difficult to pick out a Moroccan ned. I'm not sure at which point I became convinced that the meat was rat but neither of us finished it; we couldn't have or we'd have been chewing it all night.

While we were waiting for our rat to cook a group of police, doing a sweep of the streets of Essaouira, had come over to check that everything was in order and to generally impose their authority. They had clearly been wandering around with little to do and so were drawn to the fire. One of them took Amin's guitar off one of the Moroccan neds who was making a bad job of playing it. The policeman himself didn't do much better, blaming the tuning. The guitar was barely back in it's owners hands when the first few notes of 'wish you were here' rang out. The police stood mesmerised until the last few chords, when they all simultaneously realised they weren't being paid to stand about listening to music on street corners. Everyone, including them, saw the funny side of the fact they had been sucked in so easily, their 'official' front crumbling away in the process.

Amin was staying at the peasant hostel, and for some reason it sounded like a good idea to try and stay there - a decision no doubt skewed by the twelve hours of drinking preceding it! We rattled on the big wooden doors. Nothing. Again … … and then the portal window shot open, a wiry rat like face appeared. Amin and the 'gatekeeper', obviously none-too-chuffed at having been woken up, proceeded to argue for quarter of an hour before the door finally opened (arguing for everything seems to be standard practise in this part of Africa). Inside was dark; what little light there was filtered through the damp air. I could just make out the wooden rafters and earth floor which reminded me of a horse's stable or the inside of some sort of medieval castle. The gatekeeper, who was wearing a long black Berber cloak, led us up to a wooden balcony which looked down onto the main room. You could just make out lines of people sleeping on the dirt floor. Not for the first time I thought I had been transported back in time, to the medieval cities of the time of the Black Death. The room we were shown to was small and dirty. I couldn't imagine the bed sheets would ever have been changed. Some time later, just as I was dozing off, the gatekeeper returned, shouting and banging on the door of our room. He was pretty angry, and when Amin finally came round from his alcohol induced sleep it didn't take long to realise there was no point in arguing - for whatever reason he wanted me out. So I was chased out, the gatekeeper snapping at my heels with a stick all the way to the door and with no concern for those sleeping. And with one final push I was ejected, just like Oliver Twist. Outside the sun was just coming up on Christmas day.

# Falling in with the Bad Crowd

I woke in my bed at Hisham's with a hangover. I tried, unsuccessfully, to work off a thumping headache and digest the previous night's rodent burger by wandering round Essaouira's cafes.

Like the previous evening, the day snowballed chaotically on again. A crowd of us headed out to try and catch some music. The standard of the clubs we rocked up to kept dropping as we were repeatedly knocked back on account of Hisham's dreadlocks, or was it his ethnic origin? – I couldn't tell. We unsurprisingly settled on the only place that would have us. As the night wore on, it became obvious that we were becoming increasingly intertwined with Essaouira's underworld. I could probably have ducked out earlier on but curiosity got the better of me. Playing unusually well for me, I got beaten in the final of an edgy bar pool contest, loosing a bet I had made, and probably for the best, as I was in no position to start extricating money from groups of bar regulars. The so-called friends I had arrived with had left, leaving me with a bar tab which if I didn't pay, I soon realised I was going to get beaten up. But I made new 'friends', to use the term loosely, getting carried away with a fascination in it all. Hours later, after several stops off in different parts of the city, I realised that the girl I was hanging about with was a prostitute, and I decided it was time to move on. I was in a dodgy part of town and had to negotiate my return to the normal world.

For me, Morocco was characterised by the intensity of experience. The turmoil, the abrasive nature of people and the inability to trust almost anyone added to the excitement. But the experiences congealed in my brain as amazing bittersweet memories – dislike and intrigue compounded into one. Sticking to cities and missing out rural areas and the Atlas mountains probably skewed my overall perception of the country, mountains having a habit of cutting people down to size. I had experienced enough excitement though, and felt ready to leave Morocco.

On Boxing Day I pulled a whistle out of my bag, put a hat out and played some music on the street, earning myself an invitation into a café to play some more and drink tea. I watched the glum faced tourists wandering around looking for a Christmas suntan and a Moroccan vase or sculpture to sit on their mantelpiece. This is pretty much the limit of Morocco's tourist route for most Europeans. I wasn't too sure what to expect to the south of Essaouira but I knew it would be different, at least more remote, probably more extreme, and hopefully as interesting.

# Joining North and South

It's a 24 hour bus journey to Dakhla from Essaouira. The road stretches through one of the most thinly populated landscapes in the world, forming a no-mans land whose ownership has been debated for centuries and continues to be to this day. In 2001, after years of fighting between various tribal and state armies including Mauritania, Morocco, Spain and independent rebel forces, never numbering more than a few hundred in total, Western Sahara was put in Morocco's care. Polisario rebels fighting for independence had continued sporadic attacks taking the form of Wild West style hold-ups on outposts and transportation, including the iron-ore train running into the desert from the Mauritanian coast. Although the border remains mined, these attacks have subsided in the last few years. Looking at the landscape it's difficult to understand why anyone would fight over it; there's very little there to remind you that you are in fact on planet Earth, but that can only speak volumes for the dedication that people have to live in such environments, showing their connection to the land.

The bus stops in Dakhla, and from there you've got to make your own way. After some time asking around I found a lift, along with 13 others in the back of a transit van. So the 24 hour bus journey was followed by 13 hours blasting across the desert in a beaten up old transit van that had been passed for dead in Europe many years ago. There were no windows in the back, so with no view we sat in the dark, trying to find as uncontorted a position as possible. There was always at least one of your limbs which wasn't getting blood, so as long as they each took a turn, it was fine.

Heading south, the petrol stations, still barricaded like they expect war to break out at any moment, become increasingly run down as you think that each is the final outpost in the frontier land. The desert heat, the vast landscape, the burnt out cars, the vehicle convoys: my eyes rolled back in their sockets from the tiredness of continual travel and in amazement at the Mad-Max world that surrounded me.

The road slowly turns to a dirt track and you leave the northern hemisphere behind. I'm offering cashew nuts round the team in the back of the transit. I've taken enough food and water for two days but I've not got a visa for Mauritania. I thought there would be more chance of my travelling companions arguing my case at the border and less chance of being left behind, stranded, if they like me.

Perhaps unsurprisingly my travelling buddies are an interesting bunch. It's difficult to understand how such a journey could be routine for some people. Not for the first time, I'm frustrated by the lack of language in which to speak to them. Despite this we get along well as everyone was prepared to laugh at the ridiculousness of the situation, the misfortune of having to travel in such a poor vehicle, and the hopeless ineffectiveness of everything, including the road.

As if the dispute of ownership over Western Sahara doesn't give rise to enough of a no-man's land, the strip between Western Sahara and Mauritania seems completely unspoken for, with the consequence that the road isn't maintained. The area remains land mined with a recommendation to travel with a guide who knows the area. From the back of the van we can't see out, so we're entrusting the route choice to the driver, but we're travelling in convoy through the darkness, following the lights of the vehicle ahead, so you can only assume that it would blow up first. The poor condition of the road is obvious from the back of the van – as we pick our way through the jagged landscape it starts to feel a bit like being in a flight simulator – crawling and bumping our way through the boulder-field. I cannot believe it is this road that connects sub-saharan Africa to North Africa and Europe.

The rumour is that the border closes at 10pm so when we arrive at the checkpoint at 11pm we fully expect to have to batten down the hatches for a cold and cramped night in the van. But under the oil lamp in the cabin the border guard, who looked more like a bandit, took my money, stamped my passport and I didn't ask too many questions.

# Beetle in a Brawl

By the time we rocked up in Nouadhibou, the Mauritanian border-town, in our battered wagon, my bowels were at bursting point. There certainly aren't toilets in vehicles in this part of the world and so several days of continual travel had taken its toll. I was so desperate that I ended up checking into a ridiculously expensive (although certainly not plush) hotel, and then kicking myself as soon as I'd been to the toilet - probably the most expensive shit I've ever been for! At least I got a shower and a bed to sleep in.

The next morning I was at the bank trying to get some local currency – Ouguiya – when it started to become obvious how much more difficult logistically Mauritania would be than Morocco. For starters, Mauritania has no bank machines, so I had Euros hidden in various different places on me: in a wallet, a hidden hip belt, stitched into my belt and in my shoe. But even with a stash of Euros it was a mission getting Ouguiya. Queuing for an hour at a bank didn't produce any results, so I wandered out and round the streets, where it should have been possible to get a better exchange rate because of the commission the banks charge, but then on the street it's also much more possible to be done over. I was just considering my options, or more accurately, looking pretty lost, when a European looking guy appeared, introduced himself as Fritz, and asked me what I was looking for. He seemed to come from nowhere, answer my prayers, and then disappear back into the swirling sand clouds of Nouadhibou several minutes later, just like I had rubbed a lamp and a Genie had appeared. In the few minutes I knew him, the wiry Dutchman gave me a master class in how to do things in West Africa. He's one of these guys with life experience developed from devoting a life to travelling round the world; an air of calm surrounding him – both quietly assured of himself and respectful of his surroundings - like there's nothing you could throw at him that he wouldn't know how to deal with. These attributes however, wouldn't have come without a price, which is often sacrificing family life or friendships to push on out of the comfort zone time and time again. As quickly as he had arrived, he vanished, back into the desert, and I was left scratching my head and clutching a thick bundle of Mauritanian Ouguiya.

I wandered round getting a feel for the new place I found myself in - it took a bit of getting used to. Nouadhibou retains the feel of a post apocalyptic frontier town, something between the Wild West, a South American Favella, and Beirut. The town itself sits on a peninsula with one road and one railway in and out. The railway carries the world's longest train, taking Iron Ore from Zouérat, a mining town roughly 1000 miles into the Sahara desert, to the ships at the port on the coast. The mine accounts for 40% of Mauritania's Gross Domestic Product. In two weeks time Zouérat will be stowed out as the Paris > Dakar Rally comes through, which when viewing it from this side – from Africa – seems little more than a grotesque show where rich westerners drive vehicles through one of the poorest parts of the world. I'm sure it makes for good TV though.

The beaches on one side of the peninsula are land-mined or littered with oil tankers, ship-wrecked at the end of their life for insurance purposes. Disposing of oil tankers here makes sense to oil and freight companies, because the people are so poor and preoccupied with the task of survival, that they do not have the energy nor the means to launch any sort of opposition.

Off the coast a steady stream of ships carrying a payload of rubbish from Europe, which is given to African governments who are paid to dispose of it quietly. The money is pocketed by the corrupt government and the rubbish dumped on the people's land.

The sad reality is that the huge consumption of energy and goods of the 'developed' world, is paid for by Africans who have little aspiration for material wealth. Global warming will devastate Africa before anywhere else, pushing the continent's crisis to unprecedented levels. The blood is on all of our hands. It's implausible to wave a finger at oil companies as you fill your car with petrol and leave your house with a dozen appliances left on. And it's a serious, nonetheless common misjudgment to think we can continue living this way.

Nouadhibou itself is crumbling into the dust that swirls around it. The locals depend on the wind to clear away the rubbish they drop on the ground, but it collects in piles before being blown into the desert, which skinny marauding goats and chickens pick over. There is not much meat on any bone here. Food is generally an unexciting combination of ten or so different things – bread, rice, processed cheese, onion, egg, couscous, tinned fish and some camel, goat or fish if you are lucky.

As you cross the border into Mauritania the make up of the population changes and with it, the physique of the people. Despite the limited supply of food, the black Africans are generally bigger and more muscley than Arabs, or Europeans for that matter. I wouldn't like to theorise why this might be but it certainly reduces your chances in a brawl.

Having changed some money with Fritz's help, I turned my attention to finding somewhere cheap to stay, this time thinking before I needed to check in to an extortionate hotel to use the toilet. My hunt though, was interrupted by a fight across the road. Within a few seconds, there were lots of people around, trying to either provoke or break up the two men who started at each other. It seemed as if one of the men had something that the other wanted and one jumped into a barely recognisable Volkswagen beetle to make an escape. But it was only a partial get away, the other hooking his arm in through the window as the car wheel-spun off, dragging him across the loose gravel and whipping up a cloud of dust. The beetle, a skeleton of a car missing nearly all it's body panels so it's engine could be seen rattling about on the car's chassis - took off down the road. For a split second it was coming directly for me, and the scene was complete – the ghetto mud-houses, the skeleton of the car dragging the man, the dust, the sun, the heat, the look on the driver's face and the riotous crowd in the background shouting and jeering, but simultaneously transfixed by what would happen next. The scene left an enduring image in my mind. In the heat of the moment, the split second hesitation I took, thinking a photo might turn things on me or that I might get run-over, was enough to lose the picture. But I knew I should've taken it. To me these situations are something special; that one in a million event, and the image that records it - often leaving more to the imagination than witnessing the event itself. It is completely the opposite of the zillionth photo of plastic Mickey Mouse in Disneyland Florida. It might seem strange that I could find so much interest in a street fight in one of the poorest parts of Africa. Much of the world aspires to the comfortable lifestyle you might find in Florida, but suffocated to varying degrees by material wealth, it struggles to retain authenticity. Africa is seen as the rubbish tip of the world, as the problem, a model to be avoided, one that needs our kindness and our charity to keep it's flame burning, which is of course ironic given the way we have exploited it's resources. But in reality Africa has many things right which we don't; grounded in the realities of life which can so easily be glossed over in a vain struggle for 'success'.

## Push Start City

In need of some food that wasn't bread or processed cheese, I went fishing that afternoon. A street kid helped me get a taxi and ended up tagging along, presumably with the hope of making some money. The kid was young – maybe 13 – but really sharp with that kind of street wiseness that you only get from growing up on the street in one of the poorest corners of the world, a place where learning to survive on your own isn't something that happens in your late teens or twenties. I was watching him closely – partly just interested in him, and partly because I half thought the artful dodger might pull a fast one on me.

The taxi, which broke down four times on the way to the lagoon, had lots of parts missing. With an absence of starter motors in vehicles in this part of the world, pushing is the usual means of getting going. This particular model – an old Merc - only kept running with the revs maxed out, so we cruised down Nouadhibou high street in first gear with the engine screaming for mercy [some hip-hop blasting out the speakers would've been perfect had there been any, but the car had no doors, never mind a stereo system]. None of the high street 'shoppers' - herders, goats, or chickens, batted an eyelid…until the motor stalled and then they'd come running over to help with the push start; a local tradition it appeared.

This car, living it's umpteenth life after it's first in Europe, is typical of African cars. Some people make a career out of driving old vehicles – termed Euro-bangers – from Europe to Africa, forming a steady stream that provides the best chance of hitching a ride if you're heading south.

When we finally arrived at the lagoon I paid over the odds to hire a boat to go fishing – it's value to me inflated by the thought of eating another processed cheese sandwich. Fortunately the moment the baited hook hit the water, the fish swarmed around it like piranha. They were fast and strong, nothing like trout, salmon or any of the cold water fish from back home, with a short fat spine and virtually no guts, as I'd find out later during the gutting. Our guide, an old guy who looked like he'd sailed round the world several times, was baiting the hooks, first with a little squid we'd taken out with us, and then with the fish we'd just caught, picking and slicing the flesh off whichever unlucky fish came to hand, before feeding it back to their family. We caught seventeen fish in half an hour, all-be-it the kid caught more than me. I split the fish between the three of us and I gave the kid the equivalent of five Euros. He looked slightly shocked and then he was gone before I had time to change my mind. I realised that I hadn't adjusted my prices from Morocco – it's easy to calculate wrong and pay someone the equivalent of a months salary or more. Travelling like this can be little more than a collection of fuck-ups at times. As soon as you get used to one set of customs, prices and scams, you move on to make another set of mistakes. I guess that is maybe why you learn so much.

# The Sandstorm Express

It took some Imodium to get me up and running before catching the Iron Ore train going East into the Sahara. Having dropped it's payload, the train travels back from the coast empty. You can pay and fight to get a place on one of the two passenger carriages or jump into one of the empty freight buckets for free.

A ride across the desert in an open top wagon seems like a good idea at first but it doesn't take long to work out why it's free. We're at the back of a 2 ½ mile long train, supposedly the longest train in the world, and the back carriages travel through a sandstorm whipped up by the rest of the train travelling ahead of you. The sand gets everywhere - in your hair, clothes, eyes, ears, food, lungs – slowly eating away at your soul until you feel ready to lose the plot in a fit of rage. But getting angry in a sandstorm doesn't help, and the best you can do is sit with your eyes closed and some form of bandana over your face for the 12 hour journey.

To make things worse, the train has no suspension. You get no peace as the carriages rattle about, and every time the train speeds up or slows down the slack between the carriages gets taken up. With so many couplings between the carriages of a 2 ½ mile train, the slack between the front and back is big enough for the jolt, which accumulates power as it travels down the train like a supersonic bang, to throw you off your feet. Then, just to cap it all off, the night comes and the desert cold sets in.

It's hard to imagine just how poor the people are who travel this route regularly. A place in the passenger carriages costs the equivalent of a few Euros, and the locals knew what it would be like to travel in the iron ore buckets. In our bucket there were several locals, including a family travelling with a washing machine.

Very occasionally we'd get a break from the sandstorm as the train slowed down at desert crossing points.    Several hours of vibration makes it difficult to avoid going to the toilet, an operation that involved climbing over the side of the bucket and balancing on the coupling. This was usually while the train is moving and particularly difficult for ladies.

The short breaks also provided a chance for a laugh, most often at our own expense and something to do with the misery of our circumstances.  No one complained.  I shared some biscuits around and sang the Macarina to the amusement of the kids, and in return got part of a blanket to lie under when the night came in.

At 2am I climbed over the edge of the bucket for the last time and onto terra firma, leaving the train to trundle the final 3 hours on to Zouérat mining town. I didn't envy the passengers that stayed on the train, but little did I realise that we had a further 4 hour ride by bush taxi to get to the nearest town. The Iron Ore train dropped me off in the middle of nowhere; a desert T-junction where a dirt track met the railway line, but 2am was rush hour at the main transport intersection for hundreds of miles in any direction.  So there I was at a taxi rank in the desert with two Japanese folk who had also had the misfortune of catching the 'sandstorm express' – the Japanese having a lovely habit of popping up out of nowhere with a massive cheeser just when you thought you were going to top yourself.    The speed of the bush taxi ride reminded me that the Paris>Dakar rally would be coming through in ten days' time, possibly over this very terrain.   At 6am we arrived in Atâr, a place of huge historical significance in the teaching of Islam, but little more than a crumbling town today.  It was difficult to get on with the locals, and on Hogmanay morning the three of us – myself and the two Japanese folk - resolved to travel on to one of the very remote Saharan villages for the bells.   Travellers of like mind I had met in

Nouadhibou, Australians Pete and Theresa and a Czech/Hungarian couple Daniel and Marion, had planned to be in Chinguetti village for the turn of the year, so it seemed like a good idea to bash on and try and meet them.

Negiotations for a bush taxi were heated. The Hilux, which started with 6 passengers, rocked out of Atar with 22 people on board. At first I thought this was some sort of joke, to wind us up, but it wasn't. The only thing that stopped anyone falling out was the fact that everyone was packed in so tightly. Myself and the two Japanese, Novo and Suki, were sitting on top of the cabin of the pick-up. On the outside, perched on the edge just above the doors, were myself and Novo, who hadn't worked out that when we went round corners he might fall off. He panicked as he almost fell off at the first turn, but even through this his permanent smile never dwindled - only becoming more forced. I grabbed him, making us much more stable together.

It soon became obvious there was a mountain pass to overcome. Unsurprisingly, under the stain of it's payload and steepness of the road, the Hilux overheated. The lack of a handbrake meant that the mechanic, (it's bad practise to travel in the Sahara without a mechanic) had to jump out with some blocks to put under the wheels so the Hilux didn't roll backwards down the hill. It was all carried out with well practised efficiency. My hat went off to the Hilux, which seemed to come back from the dead again and again. The entire country runs on Mercs and Toyota 4x4s, apart from them and camels, little else seems to work in the desert for any length of time; the raggedy roads rattling the chassis to bits before being sand blasted to nothing.

When we finally made it to the desert village of Chinguetti, I was there barely one minute before there was a man inviting me to his family home for some food. The goat and couscous was eaten in the customary manner; with the hands from a big bowl that sits in the middle of the floor. Throughout, the entire family sat slow chewing their food whilst staring continuously at me, making it impossible to pretend to eat. There's not much of the goat that doesn't get eaten, it starts at good old fashioned meat, goes through most of the organs, then the intestines, and on to who knows where (it's better not to ask). Usually the stranger the body part the more of a delicacy it's considered to be, and therefore less acceptable to pass it up. While these eating habits might seem disagreeable to us, especially if the innards of the goat are laid out in front of you cooked though they may be, it's probably what's kept these people alive. There really isn't that much to eat in the desert, and in that regard they get my respect. I just got on with trying not to feel sick while eating.

Half way through this I realised that it was in fact a trap; feed the tourist goats' intestines and he will be obliged to buy whatever is offered to him, in this case a four day camel trek for 150 Euro. My host, Abdul, I could see, from the way he treated his wife and family, was a pretty disagreeable character, so I had no inclination to spend four days in the desert with him. Through a linguistically 'challenged' conversation he persisted in trying to get me to agree to a deal, becoming gradually more and more unpleasant as I made more and more excuses. Under normal circumstances you would tell him to 'fuck off' and wander on, but with an audience of several generations, I didn't think pulling the ejector chord and boosting out without any show of gratitude would do much for race relations, so I resolved to try and buy a smaller thing which I did want: a Seesh; a thin cotton head scarf which is invaluable for keeping the desert sand out of your hair and face. Sitting in the main room of the mud-house with little more than some pots and pans for family possessions, I was pretty surprised to hear a mobile phone ringing (mobiles seem to rank alongside camels in importance - another privilege unfortunately reserved for men). While Abdul answered it, I took my chance; paying his wife for the headscarf, thanking the family, and leaving. I could see Abdul was furious that I left, and furious that his wife had done the deal, traditionally the man's role, collecting the money in the process. It was her that had gone to the effort of cooking the meal, and therefore I felt I should reward her rather than him. The moment of hesitation Abdul took as he was answering his precious phone call was enough to get me on my way. I spent the rest of the time in Chinguetti avoiding Abdul, somewhat unsuccessfully I might add, as a small dessert village isn't an easy place to keep yourself hidden in – there's not much foliage about.

# A Desert Stramash

I had no intention of being stuck in the Sahara toasting in 2007 with myself and a tin of pilchards, although it did look like it might go that way a few times. Chasing round West Africa on your own is all very well when you're after some excitement, but there comes a time when it's good to chill out and spend some time with like minded people.

Four days previously, meeting Theressa, Pete, Daniel and Marion in Nouadhibou, I quickly realised that we were all of like mind, and made a loose agreement to meet for Hogmanay in Chinguetti. The plan worked, and after some asking about the village, I found them sitting about in a dirty auberge discussing what else they could possibly make for dinner with the only five or six ingredients available in this part of the world. We concluded that we had, in fact, used the ingredients in every possible combination, and so we went out on the 'town' (village) to get some food and celebrate the New Year incoming.

The only 'public house' was run by a French woman who had developed her own desert look – thin straggly sand blasted hair and sun bleached clothes. She didn't look all there, like she'd run away from France and turned feral in the wilds of Mauritania, and when she served us some cold omelettes it wasn't clear if she'd forgotten to heat them or this was just the way they were eaten round here.

As we sat down on the ground to eat, (unsurprisingly, we were the only customers) members of a band assembled in front of us. For the band this was a proud moment to play for some visitors to their village. There was a singer, a man on some sort of desert mandolin, and a rhythm section containing two sets of old sandals, metal pans and a broomstick. The whole set-up was amplified through a battery powered speaker measuring 6 inches in height.    I had never before considered the logistical troubles of forming a band in a village in the middle of the Sahara, and it would have been nice to say that this particular group had overcome the challenges, but it didn't turn out that way. The out-of-tune, out-of-time stramash left us wondering where to look, and as the four of us were the only audience, it would be impossible to make a sly getaway.   I've been in quite a few situations where music, struggling to hold itself together, but somehow united in it's chaos, resounds with character of people or place (admittedly there would usually be whisky involved); so I wouldn't always dismiss music on the grounds of being out-of-time or out-of-tune. Alcohol is banned in Mauritania, perhaps wisely as a desert hangover can't be fun, but it is nonetheless a very chaotic place.  Even so, we couldn't quite get into the spirit of the scene that unfolded in front of us.  Maybe it was the wailing singer or the distorted mandolin five times louder than the rest, presumably so he could hear himself through the headscarf he had wrapped around his head so many times, and so tightly, that his eyes looked like they were about to pop out. The rhythm section, a pan banging sandal slapping uncoordinated mess, probably didn't help either.  But the locals that arrived seemed to like it, dancing around like goats on speed as Ministry of Sound Chinguetti swung into action.  What a scene.  I wonder if we'd look as silly to them in a nightclub in Scotland?  We managed to make an escape before the bells.

# The Wild Eyed Children

New Year's day consisted of lounging about Chinguetti and getting used to the fact that we were in a village in the Sahara. It seems that in such out-of-the-ordinary circumstances friends are made much quicker. I find little else more gratifying than meeting someone on the other side of the world, becoming best friends overnight, and wandering about with them for several weeks through all kinds of weird and wonderful situations, usually with plenty of opportunity for laughing at your own fortunes and misfortunes. It's a common misconception that solo travelling means that you are on your own. Setting out on your own usually makes it easier to meet people, although how likely it is might depend on where you choose to go.

Pete and Theressa could be loosely classed as Australian, but had in fact spent most of their lives in other parts of the world – living, travelling or working. Working as an engineer on yachts mainly in the Mediterranean, the 3 month on - 3 month off work pattern and well paid work, made it easy for Pete to travel. Theressa grew up in Lesotho, moved to Australia, studied in Finland, and travelled in between.

Marion, a fiery, ginger haired Hungarian kept us all on our toes. Always well meant, her liveliness proved to be both useful though occasionally unuseful with negotiations in the desert. Being half Czech myself, Daniel and I got off to a good start, as we could talk to each other in Czech and share the same laugh; the Czech Republic, as with all countries I would guess, having its own style of humour. There was something strangely satisfying about standing in the desert in Mauritania discussing Chinese eating habits in Czech, but whereas Daniel's linguistic skills impressively stretched to 4 or 5 languages, mine stopped just there.

Looking across the village I found it difficult to believe that people could live here at all – the landscape is so barren with so little opportunity to grow anything. But they have done, and since well before motorised transport could ferry food about. The answer, as far as I can work out, lies with a strange looking hump backed animal. Forget about the Duracell bunny, the Camel must surely be the ultimate endurance animal. Given very little food and water, they are able to walk for weeks across some of the world's most severe landscapes, sustaining speeds of up to 25mph. They stand with a cheeky disaffected grin on their faces, like they know fine well that everyone else is going to die from thirst or starvation well before they are. But this wacky animal, known as a 'Chameau' in this part of the world, must surely be the reason that these Saharan villages survived.

Collectively the five of us hired a guide for a 4x4 tour of the Adrar region; a join the dots trip round the oasis' and villages. One stop-off, in the ancient city of Ouadane, gave a hint of the scale that trans-saharan trade had once operated on. A city now empty, and slowly being reduced to a pile of stones, leaving the imagination to envisage what it must once have been like. Pretty chaotic I would've thought - I wouldn't think transporting spices, slaves and diamonds across the Sahara would've been easy. All those stories and Disney films sprung to mind – like there should be an Orangutan hopping about from foot to foot on the crumbling buildings, or a cave full of treasures from another age. It's a place that feeds the imagination.

From the 16th century, the Trans-Saharan trade declined as boats became better and better, eventually becoming motorised. We walked about the city streets followed by a group of scraggly kids. They looked almost feral; wide eyed with a wild spark in their faces. It was difficult to tell where these desert children had come from.

On our way to visit a massive crater left by an asteroid how ever many thousand or million years ago, the track petered out to nothing. The mechanic, who had been sitting on the back of the Hilux the whole time, jumped off to let some air out of the tyres – a trick which makes life easier when driving over sand. Our driver had a strange disaffected look to him and a squint eye. We weren't too sure if this was the reason why he kept driving from side to side in a random zig-zag pattern, but for this part of the journey it didn't matter - there was nothing to crash into. What amazed me was the people that we passed roaming about in the desert. Rather than drive by them in a big 4x4 I wanted to try and talk to them and work out what on earth they were doing so far away from everything. But that wasn't really an option – we were on a 'tour' and heading for the local 'attraction'. Often it seems that you are not supposed to be there, - that driving by peasants in a 4x4 is just rubbing their faces in it. They might, however, be happy foraging in the desert looking for firewood. In fact, in reality, they probably are a lot happier than your average worker in the Developed World sitting in front of a computer screen all day. I still would've thought that they'd have welcomed some help for a few hours, but while I didn't get the opportunity on this occasion, other times when I did, I found that people's reaction to the offer of a hand was generally one of confusion. Being so unaccustomed to any sort of help from visitors, they thought they must be doing something for you – you were there to take, not give. As a visitor, it is very difficult to break out of that mould; it is so ingrained in peoples' thinking, as it is behaviour cast from a relationship developed over many centuries - from the early colonialists to the modern day tourist.

My moral reservations faded into the background when there

was interesting stuff to look at. The lunar landscape of the crater induced an exuberance in us all, perhaps inspired by the feeling that we were on another planet. The track to our final stop-off was rough and steep, looking more like a dried up alpine river bed than a road. Kudos to the Hilux as it surmounted obstacle after obstacle. Pete explained to me that the high clearance of the Hilux – an advantage in overcoming extremely rough ground – had made it Australia's most dangerous car, because the centre of gravity caused it to roll extremely easily, particularly when trying to avoid kangaroos and other Australian wildlife. I think we all then tried to put that to the back of our minds later, when our squint eyed driver was trying to overtake in a sandstorm.

Over one final mountain pass the 4x4 crawled, and we dropped down into the Terjit oasis. To us it looked amazing – you can only imagine what it would look like if you had been walking through the desert for weeks to get to it. Terjit isn't a tourist village, and the people don't spin you a story to prise some cash from you; they wave as you pass and get on with whatever they were doing with a diligence I found so often lacking in Africa.

I spotted a spectacular vantage point on a hill overlooking the village. As is often the case when there are no trees or plants to gauge distances, I underestimated the size of the mountain, but this only served to make the view from the top more impressive. For a brief moment on the way up I became worried about having sandals on, and being bitten by a scorpion or snake, but pushed the thought to the back of my mind. I scrambled up the back of the hill, because the front was vertical, so that I could sit on the edge of the rock face looking down the several hundred meters to the village, and out over the oasis, as the sun went down. It was a sublime background as a thought train carried my mind away off.

The wild journey leading into 2007 had broken down to a much gentler tempo as I joined a group of five.  With four other people you are no longer relying solely on your own judgement, and every decision is made by committee, making impulsive decisions impossible.  Being in a group you are naturally less likely to get hassle from people, and you are in a much stronger position to deal with it when you do.  It's easier talking to someone in your own language than muddling through someone else's, so ultimately your attention shifts from the world to the little group you are travelling in.

# The Sheep's Head

A day later we were in Mauritania's capital – Nouakchott. The original plan to go from Barcelona to Dakar, which had never been anything more than vague, went out the window when it seemed to me that Bamako, Mali's capital, was a more exciting proposition. Bamako sits slap bang in the middle of West Africa – at the central cross roads - making it possible to go on to Ghana, Guinea or Liberia, among other countries, or to travel up to Timbuktu.

Daniel and Marion turned to travel back to Prague through Morocco, and Pete, Theressa and myself went to the embassy to collect visas for Mali. The plan was to hitch to Bamako – there probably wasn't any other way. The road connecting the vast area of South East Mauritania is badly maintained, and supposedly prone to attacks from bandits. A distance that could easily be done in a day in another part of the world, takes four or more here. The towns on this section of the road are particularly run down. Many of the buildings, unrepaired from war, are crumbling. There is rubbish and dust everywhere, and people stare vacantly. I wasn't comfortable standing on the street, never mind taking photos. There are many more disabled people here who, in the absence of wheel chairs, haul themselves about over the ground. When Pete and myself went to get some food, there was less choice even than that of the rest of Mauritania. This is not starvation in the traditional sense of the word, it's much slower than that – gradual deprivation of nutrients over the course of several decades of a life.

The following morning, standing with a thumb out wasn't getting us anywhere till a BMW came from nowhere. Cruising through the desert in a brand new five series I felt like I was in a car advert. African villages flew by as we hit 100mph, and we sat

**The Adrar Region, Mauritania**
Stepping out in the Terjit oasis.

*Photo: P. Clausen/M. Somerville*

**Djenne, Mali**
Djenne Mosque.

*Photo: Misha Somerville*

**The Dogon Country, Mali**
The village hunter's house.

*Photo: Misha Somerville*

**The Dogon Country, Mali**               *Photo: Misha Somerville*
A beautiful chaos.

**Mali**                                   *Photo: Damien Dussut*
Deep in thought.  Misha Somerville and Peter Clausen.

**The Dogon Country, Mali**                    *Photo: Misha Somerville*

Like stepping back in time.

**Nouabidhou, Mauritania**                    *Photo: Misha Somerville*

The ground here is too hot to stand on for any length of time, so you you have hop from leg to leg.

**Niger River, Mali**                    *Photo: Misha Somerville*

An early morning river crossing near Timbuktu.

**Nouabidhou, Mauritania**                    *Photo: Misha Somerville*

A boy waits at a station to catch the iron ore train to the mining town of Zouérat, several hundred miles into the Sahara.

**Mopti, Mali**                              *Photo: Misha Somerville*
Secondhand clothes arrive at the Mopti market from somewhere else in the world.

**Niger River, Mali**                        *Photo: Misha Somerville*
The cargo boat on the Niger.

Mopti, Mali

**Lassa, Mali**      *Photo: Misha Somerville*

Table football, as found on many street corners in Mali. Needless to say they were better than me.

**Nouabidhou, Mauritania**    *Photo: M. Somerville*

A girl stands enthused, listening to a travel radio.

**Mopti, Mali**
Setting out across the Niger River.

*Photo: Misha Somerville*

**The Dogon Country, Mali** *Photo: Misha Somerville*
A Catholic church in the Dogon.

**The Dogon Country, Mali** *Photo: Misha Somerville*
Dogon villages often look like they've been thrown from the sky, landing in a random jumble.

**Lassa, Mali**

*Photo: Misha Somerville*

Three generations of a family pose for a photo. Jimmy Positive centre picture.

**The Dogon Country**  *Photo: Misha Somerville*

Exploring in the Dogon we paused for a second to catch our bearth, our guide Idrissa sat on top of a rock inspecting his carved walking stick.

**Lassa, Mali**                                    *Photo: Misha Somerville*
Balloons are only marginally more common than condoms in Africa.

**The Adrar Region, Mauritania**
Suburban Mauritania.

*Photo: Misha Somerville*

**Lassa, Mali**
A mid-day jam session.

*Photo: Misha Somerville*

**Terjit, Mauritania**  *Photo:Clausen / Somerville*
It is strangely therapeutic walking through the desert.

**Lassa, Mali**  *Photo: Misha Somerville*
From the moment he saw me he didn't take his eyes off me, not even to blink. I couldn't tell what he was

separated from our surroundings, anaesthetised by air condition-
ing and tinted glass. You could slip into a strangely brilliant trance
watching goat herders, camels and wells glide through your vision,
but as the road deteriorated, our chauffeur's shortcomings became
obvious, and it was time to wake up out of the daze.

Hamada was a young, rich Arab. His family seemed, as far as
we could work out, to have acquired their wealth from some in-
volvement with the government. Studying Law in France – a very
rare privilege for a Mauritanian – and driving a split new BMW, it
was easy to see how he could see himself as a cut above his fellow
countrymen. The problem always seemed to be someone else's
fault – believing that he should get precedence over all the other
road users: cars, trucks, goats, people, camels etc. He didn't seem
to be able to see more than 20 yards in front of the car – never the
best when barrelling over a pot-holed dirt track at 100mph. You'd
enter clusters of wild camels and it would become like some sort of
computer game to guess which way they'd step next, with the rotting carcasses of the unlucky camels lying next to the road. Fortunately for everyone, we hit a pot hole before a camel. An unhealthy
crack, and Hamada hit the steering wheel, swearing in a fit of rage.
We stopped to check the car over, it didn't look like anything was
missing, and he took up a slightly less harrowing speed for the rest
of the journey.

Ayoun, the day's end point, was Hamada's home town. He offered us a place to stay, which we took up because we didn't have
much option – getting somewhere to stay in such places is not easy.
He wanted to show us good hospitality – almost as if 'entertaining'
white guests was assuring his status amongst the wealthy classes
that he belonged to. We were uneasy with the way that the serv-
ants ran around us. They came in with water to wash our eating
hand, and we sat down to eat from a big bowl in the customary

manner.  It was while I was trying to pull what little meat there was off the bone that I realised we had been served a sheep's head – the expression on it's face preserved from it's last breathing seconds; it's tongue sticking out as it made its final cry.  I looked at Theressa, who is a vegetarian, and then back at the sheep's head. We had been served a local delicacy,  a supposed honour to be offered it, and turning it down would have been highly disrespectful. The trick was to try and look like you were eating it without actually eating it.  When he learned that we were going on to Bamako, Hamada talked about how rubbish the food is in Mali – a strange conversation to be having over a sheep's head.

It transpired that Hamada was planning to travel to Bamako the next day, as his family were there on holiday.  He wanted to get the car checked out by the local mechanics after the collision earlier, and providing that was fine, we could get a lift.  We were torn; the thought of another journey with Hamada at the wheel,  against the fact we had no other guaranteed means of transport and anything else we did get would be going half the speed.  Through the usual language difficulties we asked about the journey, which was reputably the most dangerous section between Nouakchott and Bamako. He said that the situation had improved a lot, but he had been held up at gun point making the same journey a year ago.  I started to think that travelling in a BMW might not be a good move, but even so we postponed the decision to the following day.

# The Master Bodgers

I watched the faces of the mechanics when they cracked the bonnet of the 5 series.   African mechanics are a different breed. These guys are experts in keeping cars running well past their life expectancy, with an encyclopaedic knowledge of tricks of the trade, and an unbreakable will to make a vehicle work when any reasonable assessment would have placed it in a coffin.  They had no shortage of vehicles to practise on, becoming masterfully proficient bodgers in the process.  But a twenty-first century BMW?

An oil covered mechanic stood holding a hammer as the bonnet was lifted up to reveal a mass of super-alloy boxes and pipes – packed in with hardly a spare inch.   Unfazed, the mechanics poured over the car, but soon realised that it was no use – they would need more than a hammer.  A computer, or more probably a 'local BMW dealership' was required.  Beaten by an 'improvement' in technology, we saw the funny side, but the thought crossed my mind that this incident might be the first signs of a big problem for African transport.

For us though, it may well have been a blessing in disguise – making the decision for us - we'd be heading on to Ayoun on our own, rather than with Hamada.  The lift that came to us was from an elderly man who wouldn't go any faster than 35mph, and so it was from one extreme to the other, but for the time being, we were happy.

Every so often there were road-blocks guarded by serious looking soldiers.  Often with some intimidation involved, at each of the road blocks they asked to see passports, so it wasn't clear which one might be the border checkpoint.  At one such stop, the soldiers had asked our driver to go inside the checkpoint cabin.  After he had been in there for ten minutes we started to wonder why things were taking so long. Pete and myself got out of the car, and looking across to the hut saw a soldier run past the door. There was flurry of activity, and we realised that our driver was being beaten up. We weren't sure what to do; charge in looking official and pretending to be on the phone to our embassy, or just stay out of it. In the moment we paused, the driver reappeared from the cabin, looking ruffled but with no visible signs of injury. While we couldn't be sure, the three of us harboured a strong suspicion that the trouble the driver had encountered was on account of his giving us a lift. Wise to the fact that drivers receive more money from whites than locals, checkpoint guards want a slice of the cake, demanding a cash bribe in exchange for unobstructed passage. There are times when it's better to just accept the way things are, injustices and all, and not get involved. Backcountry checkpoints in the wilder African countries, particularly as the soldiers are often drunk, may well be a place to keep as low a profile as possible.

# Bamako Boom Boom

The difference is obvious within meters of being in Mali. Suddenly there are fruit stalls lining the road, people wear colourful clothes, and music pulsates through the air-waves, emanating from boom-boxes in road side cafes and on every street corner. Mali bounces along to a beat which permeates every part of it's being, and never could this have been more obvious than when emerging from a cultural bottleneck joining Europe and Africa, North and South.

Our first stop off, Nioro, charged my spirit with it's cafés and stalls, singers and talkers, all vibrating to the music flowing through it's veins – down every road from the village's heart. It seemed that West Africa started here, but had I known that Nioro was exceptional beyond the ingrained background beat of Mali, I would've stayed for longer. I wandered about the village in a trance like state until some kids challenged me to a game of table football. Like you'd expect from kids living in a village with a football table on every street corner, they turned out to be pretty good. The laugh was on me. But I did score – once – and when I high fived my partner, it was like they all caught some sort of high five disease. The woman passing us burst into laughter as we were all high fiving each other, and I thought I'd just started a high five epidemic in Nioro.

Earlier, I'd gone on a hunt for a 'Moto' – a motorbike – something that everyone seemed to be buzzing about on. I thought about getting one for touring round Mali. It turned out to be the equivalent of about 300 Euro for a small Moto. After much humming and hawing, I decided against the plan on the basis that these small Motos are only really for short distances, the roads were in poor condition, the bike would likely be old and beaten up, and there was a complete lack of any sort of safety equipment. Pete mentioned he had got a motorbike in Mongolia and ended up flying home after a serious accident. It turned out to be a good decision – the pot holes on the 'highways' were perfectly sized for losing your front wheel.

The decision was made; I joined Pete and Theressa for the final leg to Bamako. We loaded our bags onto the bus and went off to get some food. Taking a lot longer than expected, I was still at the food stall when the bus came clattering past, on it's way to Bamako with Pete hanging out the pane-less window, banging on the side of the bus, and shouting at the driver to STOP! It's amazing how deaf an African driver can be, although engines are not quiet in this part of the world, and probably shouting 'stop!' in a language he understood would've been a more effective. In any case the scene unfolded like some sort of slapstick comedy routine, with Pete taking some time to get through to the driver as the bus bounced off down the road. I grabbed the food; some strange fried dumplings, and ran after the bus. I laughed when I thought about what would've happened if I was travelling on my own at this point.

African travel is never easy; the minibus, which we had assumed would take us all the way to Bamako, was in fact just a shuttle bus to the main bus station outside Nioro. Our place on the main bus to Bamako was far from assured, as getting a space meant fighting your way through a scrum of people, hens, goats and whatever else folk decided to bring with them, with no guarantee that you were fighting to get on the right bus.

Eventually we chugged out of Nioro bus station on to another stretch of road renowned for hold-ups. It was in fact here that Hamada had been held-up the previous year, but I thought the bandits would have to be pretty desperate to hold up this wagon;

boney chickens probably aren't top of their hit list. At any rate, we didn't see any bandits, not that I knew what to look for, but I got the impression that if they turned up we'd know about it.

We'd been broken down for several hours, hiding in the shade of some desert shrubs, before going back to the bus to check out how the mechanics were getting on. The gearbox and clutch were lying out on the road. It seemed that major surgery was under way, and as it got dark it appeared as if our African travelling companions lost the faith when they all jumped on another truck, leaving just us and the mechanics. It looked as if we would be spending the night out, and after several weeks of travelling through the desert, it seemed like we would never get to Bamako. I watched a small scorpion scuttle off as one of the mechanics lit a fire.

It turned out we were waiting for replacement clutch plates. Spare parts arrived from who-knows-where, but still the operation was far from over. Finally, the mechanics put the troublesome parts in the fire to separate two seized lumps of metal – a masterful stroke to get us back on the road. At the first village we stopped, and our African co-travellers emerged from various cafes and stalls where they had been chatting, eating or playing cards. Damn, I thought, these passengers were obviously used to break downs - we had missed our chance for a night out on the town.

By the time we clattered into Bamako that night, it had been elevated to an almost Heaven like status in our minds, with promise of all those things we had been starved of in the desert: food, beer a decent shower, etc. It was never likely to live up to it's billing, at least not the vision we had created for it. Our introduction - arriving in the bus station in the run down suburbs at 4 in the morning - was followed by an argument with a taxi driver, and then negotiations with a night porter for a room in a hotel – a conversation which lasted almost an hour. Tiredness overcoming discomfort, I dozed off on a concrete floor for a few hours.

Over the following weeks, Bamako filled my mind with a different, but no less striking picture to that which I had expected. What unfolded is a city that is exciting in as much as it is dysfunctional. Their gung-ho attitude, propagated by an unbending belief that everything happens according to God's will, absolves them from any part of improving things, leaving that responsibility to the big man himself – in this case Allah. The tribes hold less sway in the modern Africa. There is little collective thought beyond 'blood' family, and any initiative is soon suffocated under swathes of inertia. These deficiencies permeate every aspect of their lives, from the polluted smog that hangs over the city, to the razor blades they throw out on the streets for their bare footed children to run over. And so a city which could so easily help itself, doesn't, and you come to realise that it takes more than money or foreign aid to change a culture like this.

But through this turmoil emerges a city with a huge soul, a lightness of heart, and a vibrancy unsurpassed by any other city I've been in. If you're smiling, then who cares about the fact that not everything works. Everyone acknowledges you, a smile is always met with a smile, and people always have time to talk to you.

Fragments of so many of West Africa's cultures come together in Bamako, coexisting often inharmoniously, and adding to the atmosphere of excitement; from the monkeys' heads sitting out on the Fetish market stalls, to the music emanating out of open air venues and clubs: the dark spiritual meets the high spirited.

I was out on my own again, wandering around and looking for a place to stay. Eventually I got a bed to hang my mosquito net over in some sort of hostel. As I was going about the trial and error process of tying the net to anything that might hold, my next door neighbour – Marmaduke - a few years younger than me, turned up.  We talked for a bit, only sometimes over-coming the language barrier.  He started playing music through his mobile phone, and then he was singing along.  Next he grabbed me by the hand and we were dancing round the room.  When I sat down on the bed, he sat down next to me and started to run his fingers through my hair and touch my face.  Now maybe you're thinking that I didn't read the sign on the door of the hostel properly, and to be honest I was thinking the same thing – it all seemed a little strange.  In my unease I got up and made some excuse to go outside- to empty my socks of sand or something.

Thinking back later in the day it became obvious that he in fact wasn't coming on to me at all.  He was simply an innocent, enthusiastic guy.  Only behavioural differences between cultures had made me think otherwise.  It's common for guys to go round holding hands just as friends, at least in this part of Africa.  My reaction to the way Marmaduke acted seemed to show the ridiculousness of the way basic gestures are skewed in our culture, and yet we certainly are one of the most tolerant cultures with respect to homosexuality.  It seemed strange that other parts of the world, with less contorted views on basic everyday gestures, often have a much lower tolerance of homosexuality, with at worst,  punishment by death.

Out and about round Bamako, all my thoughts melted into mush as the city scooped me up. West Africa came closer than ever before, too close to contemplate, but magnificent in its experience. The sun, the sweat, the dust, the colour, the poverty, the people, all swirled into one with my tiredness and Bamako's feverish activity, as I marched for hours like some sort of tranced-out insect.

# Searching for Cigarettes

"Jimmy Positive….positive by name, positive by nature". Jimmy 'Positive' said this so many times in the while I knew him, it made me think he had murdered someone. Often the line was his starting point for a Rasta infused prophetic speech on his views of the world. An instantly charistmatic character, he could often be found right in the middle of a group of people all fascinated by his philosophical ramblings.

Originally from Burkina Fasso, Jimmy had come to Mali after a few years in Ghana – his time in the Anglophile country had meant he'd picked up some English. He showed me where to get some cheap street food, and then he said he had somewhere he wanted to take me. I got my first introduction to the Mammy Wagons – the converted ex-European Toyota and Citroën vans and pick-ups which formed the backbone of Bamako's public transport system. We travelled right out of the city to the end of the line, where the Mammy Wagon stopped to turn back, by which time it was dark. Jimmy asked me to follow him up an unlit track through the trees. I paused briefly, before stepping out after him; I didn't really know Jimmy or where we were going, but for some reason I thought it would be OK, and it was.

At the top of the hill, we came out above the tree line to see the lights of Bamako shimmering down beneath us. We carried on, a distant hubbub drawing closer until we were it and it was us. Up in the hills, away from the clamour of the city, there was a café serving eggs, bread, Nescafe, beer, and cheap wine in sachets – what more could you possibly want? We spent the night round the campfire with some of the locals, where the mission became to teach me how to speak French. My short-comings were only made up for by their inability to pronounce English words. It's amazing how much fun you can have when everyone's shit at something.

The idea of going to a nightclub floated into our heads and wouldn't leave, so Jimmy and myself took off down the hill with a sachet of cheap wine. In club Djembe we sat down to a drink that was much more bearable. A band played an African Ska-jazz-funk concoction. I asked Jimmy if any of the girls were prostitutes, he said all of them were. I couldn't get my head round the fact that girls in bars in Africa, at least in this part, were almost always prostitutes - professionals to varying degrees.

By the time Jimmy took to the dance floor, I was feeling completely whacked. I stepped outside club Djembe for some fresh air, feeling dizzy and slightly disorientated. The tiredness, cheap wine, beer and street food, all conspired against me until, after six or seven stomach churning hours, I ran from my bed at the hostel with a mouth full of sick. African toilets, little more than a hole in the ground, make for small targets for spewing into. Spending the next few days in bed, I went back to the same food stall a couple of days later, stubbornly convinced that I had developed some sort of resistance to the bug. I hadn't, and was ill again, but this time, without having drunk lots of cooking wine, there was no sick involved. I emerged in a wobbly state after several days of illness. Some girls who were staying at the hostel asked if I could play some music for a film they were making for Canadian TV about children in West Africa. After several days of being cooped up I played something I had never played before, and when pressed for a name for the credits, there were only a few words which jumped out and went on to resound through my head in the coming months – *Bamako Boom Boom*.

In Jimmy, I had a new friend to show me round the city, and we spent much of the next few weeks together. He showed me to the places I wouldn't have been able to go otherwise, and told me which streets and routes to avoid. In Lassa, the village above Bamako, we rented a concrete hut to sleep in. There was no where to hang the mosquito net in the hut, but Jimmy told me we were at too high an altitude for the mosquitoes but I wasn't convinced. It took us a few days to get any furniture, which in the end totalled two sleeping mats – we were both used to sleeping on concrete.

When I hung out with Jimmy we were always on a mission: to get cigarettes. We'd spend half an hour tracking down someone with smokes, exchange a few cents for a couple of cigarettes, smoke them and then go through the same process an hour later. The thought of buying a packet never crossed Jimmy's mind. This was a metaphor for Africa's psyche that I kept returning to.

Jimmy stops and talks to everyone, getting to know hundreds of people round the city in the process of looking for cigarettes, but for all that he makes friends quickly, he loses them just as rapidly. Jimmy Positive 'positive by name, positive by nature' suffered from stuck record syndrome. After a point, he'd stop listening, getting so wrapped up in the delivery of his ten commandments that whatever anyone else had to say wasn't important. He didn't take on any new information, and so his message, initially compelling, wore thin on the ground as he repeated himself like a stuck record. He became, without realising it, a caricature of himself. The situation was often aggravated by smoking grass or drinking cheap alcohol – because of his small size it never took long to go to his head – making his character 'phat' in all the wrong places.

We spent an amazing day wandering through the Lassa village, and amidst the excitement of the arrival of a 'Tubab' - a white person - shook the hands of thousands of smiling Africans, but then later Jimmy would be cursing the very same people, accusing them of having stolen money from his bag.

People would approach Jimmy cautiously to see what sort of mood he was in, but being with him all the time I didn't have that luxury and eventually everything started to get to me. The bouts of illness, Jimmy's constant prophesising, and difficulties in readjusting to the culture, had all unknowingly crept up on me – manifesting themselves into a horrendously bad mood in which I would blame everything but myself.

I was tired of saying 'NO!' to people. I would wake up in the morning, walk down the street, and have said 'no' thirty times before saying another word. Everyone seemed to want something, usually money, and every conversation eventually got round to that point – some quicker than others. I found my response got angrier and angrier as time went on. Occasionally I caught myself snapping at some poor street kid who put their hand out in my direction. I didn't like what it was making me into – I had no desire to be a 'no' person and it was easy to blame the people round you for that.

Before I exploded with several weeks of pent up frustration in some unsuspecting person's face, I sat in what had been my house for the last few days – a windowless concrete cabin three meters by three meters across - and tried to vent some of my anger by playing some music and writing. What came out onto the paper was, in retrospect, a kneejerk reaction, and not a carefully considered opinion, but regardless of the anger and frustration that fuelled this outburst, there may be some truth in it. It would be a lot easier for me not to mention it all, but at the same time these issues are real and important, and shouldn't be glossed over. I wrote:

*"I don't understand this continent. Why make it so difficult? If you don't leave rubbish in the streets then there won't be so many bloody flies. The lack of trustworthy people; the fact that most people are trying to deceive you into doing something that you don't want to do; the*

*fact that people eat with their hands when there's no bog roll and so many are dying from contagious disease; the fact that people don't want to help themselves."*

Utterly fed up, for the first time in my life I felt slightly home sick – never having been the sort to get home sick, it came as a new feeling.  At that moment, Scotland looked like a distant oasis – with a heavenly green glow.  I imagined walking into a pub and up to the bar, for someone to offer to buy me a pint.  The common gesture of buying a friend a pint kept returning to the front of my mind in the following weeks – although I was unsure if it was more to do with wanting a cold beer than the decency of one of our age old and commonly practised customs.

I couldn't understand it.  Any previous place I'd been to, the deficiencies had been made up for in some way – very often the poorer the place the more generous (and happy) the people.  I loved that thought and found it difficult to accept its incorrectness.  Here I realised that Africa, tinged with a desperation for survival, broke the rule.

There were undoubtedly parts of African culture which I found difficult to understand – sometimes it seemed the problems could have such easy solutions.  It is difficult not to judge the continent – it wills you with open arms to reject it to the rubbish bin, leaving you to join the colonial voices of the past.

I once watched a man trying to pour water from a plastic kettle into a mug.  With the kettle pointing directly away from him he tipped the kettle sideways so the water dribbled out the lid of the kettle and onto the ground.  He was there for several minutes before he gave up, not realising that if he tipped the kettle forwards, the water would come out of the nozzle and into the mug.  Accounts of this type litter the books of previous visitors to Africa.

But I don't believe I am committing Africa to the rubbish bin

– it is all right to criticise, every place has it's strengths and weaknesses and there's always a better way of doing things, and that goes for anywhere. People who place more value on communities and people round about them don't have to know how to use every kitchen appliance. Why spend your time making aircraft carriers when you can sit round the fire and tell stories?

And, of course, my experiences of travelling round Africa are entirely based on peoples' reactions to me as a white person. If people are not always entirely honest with me as a white, I could never claim we have been honest with them.

Bamako, at the heart of West Africa, is certainly a place that inspires the debate on Africa's wider issues. I had had my fill for the time being, and felt it was time to move on. I told Jimmy I was going to leave, spent one last night on the concrete floor and headed for the bus station.

# Up a Water Tower

There was a decision to be made. I didn't realise it at the time but it would turn out to be a pretty important one. Apart from one I had come in on, there are three main roads out of Bamako – South West to Guinea, South to the Ivory Coast or East to Timbuktu and Burkina Faso. The fact the Ivory Coast was at war with itself made the decision a little easier. The remaining routes couldn't have been much more different; Timbuktu's desert sandscape contrasting the rainforested mountains of Guinea. My eyes would be wide open whichever way I went.

From where I was standing Guinea seemed like a wild card. The rainforested Fonte Djallon mountains set it apart from it's neighbours and added one final twist to an irrepressibly complex and deep rooted West African culture. Like so many mountain ranges around the world – the Andes or the Himalayas as extreme examples – they act as an incubator of human spirit; by whittling away the chaff. The religions which come off these slopes teach respect, instilled by a feeling of insignificance in such mighty landscapes. Many that have been to the Fonte Djallon talk of their spiritual significance, the mountain stop-offs often have historical importance as retreats and places of healing. The Fonte Djallon is also home of the Djembe drum and a life affirming pilgrimage for the few hardcore drummers that attempt it.

The rain falling on these mountains has carved deep jungle canyons, forming the source of three of West Africa's major rivers – the Gambia, the Senegal and the Niger, which runs off the hills flowing directly inland for almost a thousand miles before changing its mind - and who could blame it - as it hits the Sahara desert at Timbuktu and meanders back towards the Nigerian coast. The roads and vehicles which navigate the Fonte Djallon are hazardous at best. The trucks, which often overturn, form obstacles in themselves, and the landslides mean that you can never be sure what's round the next corner. Cars in Guinea have come one stage further down the chain again - being bought secondhand from Mali or Senegal; while in Mali they typically carry seven (a driver, two to the passenger seat and four in the back), in Guinea it's standard practise to carry nine. Guinea borders, amongst others, Liberia, Sierra Leone and the Ivory Coast, taking on huge numbers of refuges from these war torn regions. The average life expectancy in Guinea is 50.

With the World's second largest supply of Bauxite – a key component in the manufacture of aluminium – Guinea's poverty is avoidable, even despite the strain placed on it by neighbouring countries. The president, Lansana Conté, has remained highly unpopular since he instated himself in 1984 – remaining there courtesy of several extremely dubiously fought elections, the last of which was boycotted by the opposition parties. His corrupt and idealistic approach has done little for his country.

Guinea painted a wild and vivid picture in my head. One step further off the beaten track, I was convinced that here there would be much to see and learn, but Timbuktu seemed so close – at least if I was some sort of bird I might have made it in reasonable time, but African transport is not renowned for its speed. So I decided that I'd go to Timbuktu before returning to Bamako and then on to Guinea. It was a decision that turned out to be a lot more important than it seemed at the time.

As it was, it took me a day's bus journey and four days on a cargo boat up the Niger River to figure out that Timbuktu was in fact just a tourist trap, and I, like so many others, had gone there for all the wrong reasons – just to say that I'd been there. As I found out, part of the mystery surrounding Timbuktu is because there really is very little there now. The tourists generally stick to 4x4s, occasionally piling out to take photos. Like sheep, as soon as one person takes a photo of something, they all do so as not to be outdone. I don't think they actually knew what they were photographing – they certainly didn't ask anyone.

I decided to climb a water tower. Half way up I started to question my plan; perhaps unsurprisingly ladders always seem to get more difficult as you get higher. I avoided looking down until some locals started shouting at me. I looked up to see how much further I had to go and spotted four or five owls higher up on the ladder where it was enclosed by the water tank. Just at that second a volley of owl shit rained down on me. I laughed at the absurdity of the situation – covered in owl shit and stuck half way up a water tower in Timbuktu – I had just wanted a good view from the top of the Water Tower. In any case it became obvious that climbing back down would probably be a good idea.

Such was Timbuktu – you've got to make your own entertainment. Fortunately I had good company; I'd met a French guy Damien on the cargo boat, and had been sharing laughs and hassles since then. Later on I was playing some music – a few tunes on the whistle, out on the roof of one of the village's mud houses. As it turned out Damien was a really good juggler and there was soon a crowd of people watching us. They stood keeping a distance, watching us like we were some sort of wild animal, until one little boy plucked up the courage to come closer. He walked slowly, stopping every so often until he was up on the roof and a few yards away from us, and there he stayed - mesmerised - while the others dared not come any closer. Although interesting to me at the time, I didn't realise how much this little experience might influence and inspire ideas in the future.

On a more practical note, I had some issues to deal with. The last opportunity I had to use a bank machine had been way back in Morocco – Mauritania didn't have any bank machines and the only other bank machine, in Bamako, wouldn't accept my card. Expecting this problem I had cash stashed in various places on me – stitched into clothing, in secret pockets, money belts and in my shoe. The trouble was, when I reached for the money in my shoe it wasn't there. Convinced that someone had stolen it, I thought back on the times I had my shoe off – trying to work out what might've happened. It wasn't till a few weeks later that I learned from another traveller who had the same problem, that putting money in your shoe isn't a good idea, as it works it's way out as you walk. I'd left a trail of Euros across Africa. The only option left was to put a phone call through to my folks and have money transferred to me by Western Union.

Like most of Africa, Timbuktu has more than it's fair share of begging. The children trail around the city with an almost constantly out-stretched arm. The tourists who oblige, revel in their own supposed generosity but are, unfortunately, completely unaware of the consequences of their actions. In Mali, to give a dollar is like the equivalent of a day's work. Even if that kid only gets something from every tenth tourist they ask, it's still enough to make a career in begging much more profitable than agriculture. In this way the ignorance of a few tourists proliferates the begging problem and suppresses the work ethic of the next generation, who might otherwise be able to make food for Africa. Here-in lies an important lesson in Africa - that throwing money at problems, on whatever scale, can inflame things as much as it can solve them. There are more effective ways and means of giving – whether it be giving pens to a local school or helping dig a well.

Tourism is not, however, all bad news for Africa. As an example: Mali had been plagued by a series of small scale – almost tribal – conflicts, fought because the minority groups didn't feel their interests were being represented by the central state government in Bamako. In the North, around Timbuktu, and deep into the desert, the Nomadic people known as the Touareg were one such group who orchestrated hit and run attacks on official government outposts. These battles went backwards and forwards as Mali, like many African countries now, struggled to maintain any sort of unity within its borders. But as tourism became the country's biggest earner, the Malian government realised something that many African governments are yet to realise: that the highly distinctive makeup of the minority groups and tribes, from their genetics to their customs, is of huge touristic and therefore economic value to their country. The Touaregs, the original camel train people, are much better looked after in Mali now, and can be seen on posters all over the country, have their culture celebrated through world renowned festivals, and no longer feel the need to fight.

Damien and I met a couple of Touaregs wandering around Timbuktu; they invited us round for a cup of tea, and as they went through the customary ritual to prepare the tea, three generations of their family sat staring at us. Their tea is drunk from small glasses – perhaps because of a lack of water in the desert – and is very sweet. It's cooked up in a small metal pot, poured from a height and re-poured from glass to glass to froth it up. The glasses are passed around so everyone has some. This is a ritual which is taken very seriously – it would likely be taken as impolite to leave before the tea runs out or before you've had at least two or three glasses, and there's usually no reason to leave. It's a time to talk in whatever language or by whatever means, and the tea is good; its sweetness providing a much needed energy boost from the desert sun-induced lethargy. I got pretty addicted to it in the desert, but maybe it was just a continuation of a tea drinking habit from back home.

As is often the case in Africa, a gesture like this is used to soften you up before the hard sale. Sometimes the only way to avoid any bad feeling is just to refuse their initial gesture and miss out on the tea and conversation. In this case, our newly found friends produced some Touareg jewellery. It can be difficult to tell who actually made it – they always claim it was them, but you can't be sure the money makes it into the hands that did the work. The Touareg jewellery really is brilliant though – the desert obviously provides the right materials and inspiration. The two men laid out their work on the ground – one set clearly crafted to a higher standard than the other, making us think that these had been made by the men themselves, rather than bought in. Damien bought a piece from the better set and as I thought it would be unfair to buy two pieces from the same person, I declined.

# The Fruit Chopper

Spotted while we were a mere speck on the horizon, you could hear the children shouting 'Tubab! Tubab!' almost before you could see them. It was a few days since we left Timbuktu, and Damien and myself had decided to climb a mountain we'd seen from our stop-over village - Douentza. We had however, completely misjudged the heat of the mid-day sun, the amount of water we needed and the scale of the mountain – a total cock-up of strategy – but the people we met on the way back made it worth-while. The fact we had slightly stupidly attempted to climb the mountain had taken us off the beaten track, so we were unexpected visitors to a village. The initial shout of 'Tubab!' drew everyone's attention, and the children came running out to meet us, all of them wanting to touch us and shake hands, running and dancing about in excitement. By the time we reached the village there was practically a festival happening – I don't think I've ever seen a happier group of people. The adults, however, had a very different reaction - standing back with a stern look on their faces - but even so, a smile was always returned with a smile.

Leaving the village with an entourage that gradually faded off, we wandered on. The landscape – typical of the Sahel – is desert like but with a greater proliferation of shrubs and trees. One such tree is the Baobab – 'the tree of life' – and in a landscape where survival is often based on ingenious use of whatever the land yields, this really is a tree of life. It can hold hundreds of litres of water which, unlike cacti, can be tapped in dry seasons. The leaves are used for condiments and medicines, the fruits are rich in vitamin C, and can be eaten or left to dry out and sucked like a sweet or added to water to make a lemonade drink. Virtually every part of the Baobab can be used to make something: soap, necklaces, glue, rubber, food flavourings, cloth, rope - you name it.  Some of these trees are over two thousand years old – time-morphed into weird and wonderful shapes and sometimes hollow, which can provide shelter for humans or animals.  I like them because they've got the most random branches, which are short and stumpy and without leaves, so it looks like a giant root sticking up in the air, or the most out of control hair style you can imagine.  The Africans have theories about how the tree was turned upside down and stuffed back in the ground so it couldn't complain anymore.  Superstitions have it that if you pick a flower of the Baobab you will be eaten by a Lion, but if you drink water that the seeds have soaked in you will be safe from crocodile attack.  The Baobab has retained its central place in communities, used as a meeting place for discussion and telling stories.

We walked on and were drawn towards a pile of luminescent green fruit – each bigger in size than a football.  And next to them in the shade of a tree sat a man measuring and chopping the hard shell of the fruit with expert precision.  First they would be measured round the outside with string, then marked and chopped with a saw like machete before being hollowed out and dried in the sun – a procedure which took half an hour.  This was his job, and the semi-circular bowls would be used for storing grains, vegetables or water.  The two halves of this particular fruit though, were gifted to us, and Damien and myself walked back across the Sahel with the bowls over our heads.  It was the kindest gesture I experienced in Africa, and we each carried the two parts of the bowls around the country, eventually taking them back to our respective homes in Scotland and the French Canadian Island Saint-Pierre & Miquelon.

# Unexpected News

I'd spilt some sardines on my trousers two days before, so it was time to wash some clothes. Sitting with my feet up waiting for my clothes to soak in a bucket, I was footering about with my travel radio when I caught the BBC World Service. The news came through in sporadic bursts of reception, but soon had my full attention. Guinea was on general strike, and people had taken to the streets in protest of president Lansana Conté – following 20 years of incompetent, self-centred and idealistic leadership of the country. Conté, of course, had control of the army and in response declared martial law, imposing curfews which left a narrow window of just a few hours of each day in which people were allowed out on to the streets. Twenty nine had been shot dead in the capital but the workers unions held firm – the strike continued. A frenzy of panic buying had exhausted food supplies, and as petrol ran out all road transport ground to a halt, breaking distribution chains and making re-supply of food impossible. Guinea started to fall apart at the seams, it's future dependant on who would crack first. Would Lansana Conté stand aside? Would there be a coup, with someone from within the army wrestling power from Conté? Would the people resort to armed resistance? I couldn't help thinking that all it would take was one arms shipment for Guinea to go the same way as neighbouring Liberia and Sierra Leone. I'm sure someone would be working on it - arms dealers do good trade in this part of the world.

Such situations must be unimaginably harsh for people. Coming from a culture of apathy, where the closest thing to a protest is 'going down the football' on a Saturday afternoon, I find it difficult to imagine what it must be like when you and everyone you know has to fight so hard for something with so little hope. A part of me wanted to be there, to see it first hand – to be amongst a group of people who all unanimously believed in one thing enough to risk their lives in taking to the streets. I knew that had I decided to go to Guinea instead of Timbuktu, I could so easily have been there just as the trouble kicked off. I wanted first hand information and ran about Douentza in the vague hope of finding an internet café. There was more hope here though of buying a camel (going rate 300-500 Euro, although I didn't go through the process of haggling for one).

For the time being there was nothing to do but get on with life in Mali, and that started with a bus ride back to Mopti in the back of an old converted Mercedes van, about the size of a Transit, along with about twenty-five other people, chickens and goats. Despite our by-now almost constant awareness of being ripped off, Damien and myself were done over as we tried to negotiate reasonably priced bus tickets. It was a trick we'd seen before; the person who claimed to be the driver was in fact just a random person, who kept half of the fee for himself, handing the rest to the real driver. Even so, avoiding this scam was difficult, as there was no way of knowing the going rate for the journey or identifying the actual driver (they certainly don't wear uniforms).

For half an hour the argument raged as the driver and co-driver/conductor tried to get more people into the van. It was of course in their interest to fit as many paying passengers in as possible, but as it was, there was hardly a spare inch. Spaces between adults were packed out with children, with chickens squeezed in between them and under the benches. On the roof was our luggage, some goats, the mechanic and the luggage boys – responsible for loading and unloading at the many stops. There were no fixed seats as such, just some wooden benches that were arranged round the outside of the rear compartment so everyone was sitting facing in and towards each other. We rattled across the desert with Phil Collins blasting, distorted, out of the bus speakers. The tape, probably courtesy of a charity hand-in scheme, was the most unlikely choice; the deep-set, weathered faces of these wiry desert characters sound-tracked by 80's stadium rock. When a child woke from sleep, he panicked and turned to his mother, horrified that he was so close to two white people. Everyone laughed, and the arguing about earning a place on the desert bus was forgotten about. Such laughs are priceless. To be in such a different place in adverse conditions and to share a laugh goes beyond language, culture and race to the realisation we are all human.

# Simple Living

The disaster-prone travel induced by these parts of Africa could leave you wondering why you were there in the first place, but every so often someone, something or somewhere turns up to amaze you. You can never tell when this might happen – sometimes the most supposedly brilliant things are in fact pretty average, but conversely the most astounding experiences can arise from nowhere, shooting your spirits upward, and in the process making you feel more alive. It's also impossible to say in which way you'll be amazed. Experiences come at you sideways to bring about realisations you could never have predicted, leaving you to track a meandering path in search of elusive goals of amazement, inspiration and realisation. While these experiences are subjective – as they say beauty is in the eye of the beholder – great places and things are undeniably bewildering to all. Whether it be the Ganges river or Macchu Picchu, appreciation and celebration weave their way into the fabric of the people. You can of course have similar experiences in day to day life, but familiar surroundings and the prescribed nature of living a routine, lessens such occurrences.

The Dogon Country is one of the places that scoops you up. After weeks of wandering around thinking that nothing in Africa works as it should, to come out into such a place as the Dogon, where everything seems to work in such simple harmony, makes you think that this is the way everywhere should be. It's easy to stand here and question why we ever needed all the extra stuff we now use in the western world, although that might be romanticising the simplicity of life here. They have their own problems, and while I stand amazed at them, they do the same in the opposite direction.

Four days spent walking around the Dogon country was only just enough to get an idea of what Dogon life is like. At one of the many stops on our walk we paused and I took a photo of our guide, Idrissa, sitting on top of a rock with the Bandiagara Escarpment, home of the Dogon, stretching out in the background. Hundreds of years ago these cliffs, jutting up hundreds of meters out of the desert, were the home of the Tellem Pigmies, who had plastered mud huts onto the cliff faces hundreds of meters up which were well enough built to withstand several centuries – the walls and windows still clearly visible from the ground. There's nothing like some gravity defying pygmies to get the imagination going. As I looked up, Idrissa smiled at my bemused expression – 'Magic' he said. The fact that climbers in recent decades, fully equipped with modern equipment, have not managed to reach some of the huts is not only testament to the Tellem's climbing ability, but also their ingenuity in building in such precarious positions.

The Tellem must have had a pretty good reason to build houses so high up – avoiding fierce animals or maybe, being small, they were just rubbish at fighting. It was assumed by the Dogon, that the houses were homes, but they were in fact only used as grain stores and tombs for dead bodies – many of the huts are still full of Pygmy bones. No evidence of where the Tellem actually lived has ever been found.

It is the escarpment that makes this place so fascinating. Like a massive naturally formed castle, the cliffs and rocks protected the people as various empires washed over the land around them. On one occasion the Dogons, fleeing from the Egyptian emperor's forces, were trapped between the ensuing army and the Niger river. The Dogons however, escaped across the river with the help of crocodiles. Now, as repayment, the Dogons keep the crocodiles in the village of Borko, where they are allowed to roam free and pester visitors for food.

Idrissa, the Dogon man with the big grin, took us – Damien, Taro (Japanese) and myself - through the Dogon for several days. We walked from village to village, occasionally hitching a ride on a cart. A cow, rather than a donkey or horse, struck me as a strange choice of animal to do the pulling - it struggling under the load. These poor cows however, were pretty much the only thing that did seem out of place in the Dogon. It seems that everything here is beautifully simple, evolving slowly and deliberately over centuries. The communities are underpinned by a structure in which everyone plays an important part – from the young, right the way through to the old, who as a celebration of their experience of life, gain status as village elders. Passage through the Dogon is made much easier with a supply of Kola nuts to barter with, a delicacy much revered by the elders. I remembered it had taken me a while to get used to the taste of whisky, so I kept trying the Kola nuts, but didn't quite manage to 'acquire' a taste for them.

We passed a well-digging operation, and going by tradition, offered the Elders, who were basking in the shade of the nearest Baobab tree, some Kola nuts. In theory I think the elders were supposed to be overseeing the operation and offering advice, but in this case they seemed to be happier taking the piss out of the younger men every time something went wrong.

It was often the kids that would show us round the villages:- Ende, Kani Kombole and the excellently named Djiguibombo (Jiggy bombo). It was turning dark one night when we heard a group of children singing. We followed our ears to the village square and when the children realised they had an audience they put more into it. They were one of the best choirs I've ever heard and they sung African songs infused with funk, soul and gospel – it was of course Africa that these genres grew from. I'm sure we don't give Africa the credit it's due for it's influence on music.

It's not all sweetness and light in the Dogon though, in fact it's pretty much as dark and sinister as your imagination can go. Much of this centers around the 'Hogon', a mean looking Sorcerer who lives away from the villages on his own, in a hut on top of the escarpment. His job is to deal with the evil spirits and keep the gods happy. Until recently it was his responsibility, following a year with a bad harvest, to deal with children donated, one from each family, as a sacrifice to appease the gods.

Dogon art and sculpture does a good job at twisting the lighter and darker elements of Dogon life into one form. Of course, in past times the best examples were carted off to museums and private collections in Europe when we whites plundered Africa.

# To Go or Not

Mopti was a high contrast to the slow pace of Dogon life. When I passed through Mopti on the way to Timbuktu previouly, I had stayed with Touré, a young guy I'd met while wandering round the town. He'd been really good to me, and in fact was one of the very few people in Africa who didn't ask me for anything, even though he'd given me a place to stay. I offered to get him some food many times, but he declined - I couldn't work out if this was just because he ate so little (it is amazing how little Africans can survive on). He'd shown me round the slums, and by boat we travelled over to the boat builders yards, which were turning out massive seventy foot wooden open canoes for transporting goods up and down the Niger – just like the one I had taken to Timbuktu several weeks earlier. It seemed strange to me that he didn't have any kind of job. Later on he explained, like many young black men he pointed out round Mopti, that he had a 'sponsor'; Touré was being paid by an older French woman to have sex with her. The comparatively rich French women pay something around 50 Euros a month, sometimes throwing in extras like a motorbike, for the privilege of fucking a young black man whenever they visited Africa. The 50 Euros was enough for Touré to live on – and the fact he was the most upfront decent guy I met in Africa seemed a contorted reality.

Back in town I was interested in some first hand information from the ground in Guinea. Hunting down reports on the internet I found a few panicked tourists who were unnerved by the curfew, the shootings, limited food supply and the suspended air travel. One more experienced traveller was less worried – pointing out that for the time being it was just the army who were armed, and the last thing they wanted was to draw the world's attention to the conflict by shooting a westerner.  I had no doubts that Guinea would be an interesting trip, but the practical difficulties seemed hard to measure from a distance.  The stand-off continued.  The Unions repeated demands for Lansana Conté to stand down and, with the general strike holding, that meant transportation around Guinea, as well as air links in and out, were severely crippled.  The longer the stand off went on, the worse the situation became.

I was torn – Guinea was the place I had most wanted to visit in West Africa, and going to any other country would've been an anticlimax – but from where I was, I couldn't even tell if the border was open.   Disappointedly I gave up on Guinea and booked a flight back to Europe to leave from Bamako.

Just the following day the news from Guinea changed.  A chink of light had broken through the dark cloud that had been hanging over the country.  The persistent pressure, mounted by the people through the Unions as a reaction against decades of poor government and extreme poverty, looked to have eroded Conté's command, and he agreed to hand power over.  The strike was called off, but none-the-less, Union leaders made it clear they were ready to resume if Conté's pledge was not met.  The country was stuck, teetering between war and peace, but with a new found hope.  I wanted to be there to see the people as they stood and won, and the opportunity to travel down through Guinea stared me in the face.  It was a chance to record in picture the peoples' victory, and a seminal moment in the country's history.

Back in Bamako I was on a mission, from Mammy Wagon to Mammy Wagon running round the city under a blistering sun.  Being inside the Air Morocco bureau, I couldn't believe I was in Bamako – the office interior had an anaesthetising effect, insulated from the chaos outside.  I fumbled around for French words to change the flight to fly from Guinea Conakry rather than Bamako, and was told it would be possible.  At the Guinea Embassy the officers informed me they could see no reason why they couldn't issue me with a visa – in fact they brushed off my questioning of the current situation, and proclaimed any suggestion of the fact the border might not be open as ridiculous.  I realised however, that they had a vested interested in collecting the 100 Euro from me, so they might be the wrong people to ask.  I wouldn't get the visa till I was absolutely sure the flight was changed.

Back at Air Morocco we went through the details, and the assistant hit 'enter' on the keyboard… and that should have been it – one flight from Guinea Conakry to London Heathrow – but it stalled, and after 3 attempts we realised that it was not allowing the flight to be changed.

Back, outside the air Morocco office, I stood at a busy junction with the usual quantities of animals, heat, dust, kids, bikes and cars screaming past.  Looking up to the sky, I wondered what to do next- fly back to Europe, keep trying to change the flight, or just forget about it and go to Guinea anyway.  I put the decision off and decided to go to a music festival.

# The Final Straw

By the time I reached Segou the following day, some 4 or 5 hours from Bamako, I was sweating like an onion in a frying pan. This itself is not an uncommon sensation whilst travelling in an African bus, but when my neck became stiff and I started to become dizzy the alarm bells started ringing – malaria?  Suddenly everything became a bit of a struggle.  The Festival chaos was not the best accompaniment to the illness.  Asking around, it soon became obvious that no-one really knew what was happening – typical of Africa really – so I walked straight to the festival director's office. The French Lady, who was clearly the lynch pin in the ram shackle set-up trying to make the party happen, quickly understood my problem and that I'd need somewhere to stay.  Myself and some others were driven round to a house which had obviously been taken over as accommodation for the festival.  I was shown to a concrete walled room with no windows and a dodgy lock.  It had the feeling of a room you might go into and never come out of, so I collapsed on a couch in the hallway, oblivious to anyone coming in or out of the house.  Neither did I have the energy, or see the point in putting up a mosquito net – rightly or wrongly.

Having met a few people who had come through malaria ok I didn't see too much reason for concern.  From my limited knowledge all but a few strains are treatable, with these having evolved over time to become resistant to many of the drugs.  I had heard of another traveller doing a similar route to me, who had fallen ill and died 24 hours later – although it's always difficult to gauge the truthfulness of these rumours.  Although I was in an area in which the 'super' strains of malaria existed, their limited prevalence made the probabilities of catching one relatively small.  Sadly the crippling effect of malaria on the continent of Africa is largely down to not taking basic precautions, and the unaffordability or absence of basic healthcare.

I was lying on the couch for long enough, maybe a day or two (the fever making time calculation difficult), before someone realised there was something wrong with me. It was a dark African schoolteacher – Maiga - who woke me. He had about as much English as I had French, but much didn't need to be said. I explained what I thought was wrong and he offered me a lift to the Hospital. On the back of the moped, my head rolled about as I tried to concentrate on staying on the bike. The journey seemed to take forever, but eventually we made it.

Progress through the hospital was like a game of snakes and ladders. It seemed to be based on bribing people, but you couldn't be sure who was who or where you were trying to get to - there certainly weren't any signposts. You'd pick the most official looking person to speak to, spend an age fighting through the language barrier just for them to disappear, leaving you with little idea if they had understood, or even if they were going to come back.

My overriding desire was to sleep, and so anytime progress stagnated I'd find a space on a floor somewhere in the hospital to lie down, any kind of space - I wasn't fussy - and within seconds I'd be away. If it wasn't for a kid that Maiga had left with me to help me through the process, who kept waking me up, I might never have made it out of the game of snakes and ladders.

Eventually I found the right department to get a blood test. I checked the needle was fresh and shortly after fell asleep on a hospital bed for however many hours – I have no idea.

When I woke up there was a man at a desk, shuffling papers and occasionally looking over the brim of his glasses at me, but not saying anything. Maiga appeared – how he found me I have no idea – and signalled it was time to go. I was confused. I expected something more, some sort of treatment, but that was it. On the way out Maiga explained, in a short conversation, that the doctor had said I had  malaria. All that effort just to be told something I already knew.

Back at the house, I fell asleep on the couch in a split second. The wasted effort didn't seem to bother me any more, nor did the fact that I hadn't eaten in several days, nor the fact I had malaria. All I wanted was to sleep – life there was a lot less painful – no headaches, no stiff neck, no fever and no pain.

Fortunately an older French woman, Sofie, took an interest in the person that had been lying asleep on the couch for so long. She woke me every so often with some water and a banana. The trouble being, it was impossible to hold anything in. I'd take a sip of water, the smallest sip, and thirty seconds later I'd be running for the shitter, for a seemingly endless cascade of green slush to come gushing out my ass. Explosive ass and African toilets make a poor combination. The floors of these toilets are usually slanted so that the 'excess' can drain away, but in this case, by some inexplicably bad planning, the toilet drained into the next-door shower cubicle. So rather than have the shower drain through the toilet, cleaning away the shit, all the shit flows through the shower cubicle. I say shower, but that's misleading - I really just mean bucket of water.

It was while squatting over this toilet at 4am that I realised I would have to try and get my act together somehow. I was losing weight quickly – at this rate I'd wither away to nothing. No-one around me spoke English or had any reason to care about me, and no-one back in Scotland knew I had malaria.

At some point later in the day I was woken by Sophie and Maiga standing next to the couch, talking about me in French. In a strange kind of round-about way I was quite glad that they looked concerned. In a broken conversation Maiga explained that he would go and get a special doctor 'for white people', but I would have to pay for it.

A doctor arrived a few hours later and I handed over the equivalent of 10 Euros. Right there, the 10 Euros that so many Africans couldn't pay. I got a once over and the Doctor explained that malaria attacks the digestive system and that I would need to eat to get better. He would give me an injection and I would need to eat as much as possible for as long as possible. Covered in sweat and shit, embarrassment wasn't foremost in my mind when the doctor stuck a needle in my ass. Whatever was in that syringe turned things around. It seemed to convince my body to hold on to the food.

Over the next few days my condition improved, but my neck became extremely stiff. Strangely now, more than before, I worried about what was going to happen. I realised this illness, whatever malaria is, was a lot more resilient than a common cold, and could possibly metamorphose and come back stronger still. It felt like it had gone back to base, was storing up it's ammo, changing tactics, and would be rolling out for phase two of the battle – where the battle ground was my body and I could only stand on the sidelines and watch.

But it didn't come back, and I had two days to make the flight from Bamako. Any immediate desire to go to Guinea disappeared. I was totally whacked and I had just two days to make the flight. The bus to Bamako, a taxi ride to the airport, check-in, security, and I stepped onto the aircraft, sat back in my seat and was asleep in a few seconds. When I woke up in Heathrow, Europe would not seem quite the same as before.

# More Than I Bargained For

Several days after I got back from Africa I was at a party in Glasgow having a drink with friends. I thought to myself, 'well, that was a hell of a week'. It seemed amazing that I was sitting where I was, a week after being in Hospital in Mali.

I started back working – on a project to make a new musical instrument, getting gradually more and more involved until almost all my time was spent thinking and making. While all this was going on, something else quietly crept up on me. I was finding it difficult to focus my mind on things, had headaches, occasional dizzy spells, nausea, pains from my chest and couldn't see properly. Six months of blood tests at the tropical disease centre, heart monitoring, and going to see various doctors didn't lead anywhere. There were no explanations and, as they said, no point of going back to see them.

Some months later, and after doing some research of my own, it became obvious that I had M.E. - or Chronic Fatigue Syndrome - possibly as a knock-on result of the malaria. M.E. an illness which doesn't show up on any sort of modern-day medical test, and as I discovered, many doctors do not recognise it – although there are millions of people who have it, and plenty of books putting forward possible explanations. Having been party to African healthcare, I felt less inclined to go on about the misgivings of ours, but even so this didn't help with the difficulty of knowing how to treat it. Where do you start with something that is so complicated that modern medicine offers no accepted explanation? What was most difficult about it is the fact that you don't know what to do to get better, and there seemed to be little or no logic as to when you felt bad.

Unlike the malaria, which was pretty much over in a week, M.E. hangs over you like a dark cloud for months, and then years, removing the ability to do things and see people:– the things which make you *you*.

The result is you end up lying on your back staring into space, unable to watch TV or read a book because your eyes can't take it, hardly leaving a room for months, and when you do, finding it difficult to walk more than a few yards. For many, depression sets in, which then exacerbates the problem, causing a downward spiral to the point that people can end up in bed in a darkened room for the rest of their lives. So with the hope of getting better, or at least not getting any worse, resting with positive thinking, it becomes a psychological battle with yourself – to tell yourself that you are OK, that you will not spend the rest of your life like this, and to try and put to the back of your mind the fact that your life, as you knew it, is no longer there. It's a battle that takes up every waking minute of every day - the biggest challenge I've been through, with some very dark days.

Over time I was to find out, with the discovery of Mickel Therapy, that the best way of getting better was to do almost completely the opposite of what is advised by the medical profession.

I never meant to write this story, and obviously I never meant to get ill – twice - but when I was ill for the second time, I realised that I needed to do something to keep myself occupied, something that wouldn't aggravate the illness  – so that I could stay positive and stand some chance of getting better. So with the scribbles I had written down in a small book, I started writing to pass the time, to re-live some of the experiences and to give myself time to think about Africa.

# Thinking Back

It's not that there was anything particularly pulling me to Africa; more that I wanted to experience something different – to see the flip side of the coin. Like most kids in the western world I grew up in comfortable surroundings – central heating, TV's, supermarkets, cars etc. – but perhaps naive about how the world works; where electricity comes from, where our rubbish goes, where our food comes from and how it's made. I thought, that of all places, Africa might teach me something about the world.

It was in Timbuktu that I realised what I did not come to Africa for; the rows of disaffected tourists snapping pictures as holiday souvenirs, simply to say they had been there. They had little interest in what Timbuktu was about, or giving anything back to make it a better place. For some reason it was the camera that defined it for me - the way people approached taking photos and the reaction of people to pictures being taken – to stand with an out-stretched arm and look as bedraggled as possible (and usually succeeding). This seems almost the complete polar opposite of many people's reaction to having photos taken in the Western World, which is to pull on a smile, completely removed from how they actually feel, and thinking only about how they look in the photo.

So I didn't think I was going to get much from a place where things seemed false. I was looking to find authentic people and places, and that seemed to mean going to poorer and poorer countries, those often affected by war.

It was crossing into Mauritania, where the people are some of the poorest in the world, that it was most obvious – the washed up oil tankers and the rubbish being shipped from Europe to Africa.

It seems that you learn more in the backwaters of the world – the places that no-one is watching.

Everything looks completely different from the other side - it's obviously a lot easier to forget about disease and starvation when it's not affecting you.  It becomes more obvious that as humans, we've been using the world's resources carelessly for tens of thousands of years, and only now are the consequences being realised – our generation is at the tipping point.  In the future, people will look back on this as a time of abundance – when almost anything was possible – the age when energy was virtually free; the time when we had oil.

It might be difficult to predict how this will play out. Will we pull together to beat the biggest challenge faced by mankind yet, or will everyone turn on each other as resources dwindle?  One thing is for certain however, it is Africa that will be worst affected.  Sadly it's the person in the desert foraging for a little firewood, food and water who will be left high and dry, they who had nothing to do with the transportation, industrialisation or computerisation that contributed to global warming. The deserts are spreading, and that makes Africa's outlook bleak.

But when it wasn't around me anymore, I missed Africa.  I got back to Glasgow and the people on the streets looked lifeless, filing glum faced in and out of chain stores.  You couldn't just stop, smile and speak to anyone.  The people, the colour, the music, the vibrancy; it seemed that for all their troubles, there was more life in West Africa.

Proceeds from this book will be donated to the Hand in Hand charity – www.handinhandinternational.org.uk. The Hand in Hand Charity is pioneering a new form of aid to developing countries; they offer low interest loans and business support to people in some of the poorest parts of the world who want to start their own businesses – undercutting local loan sharks and encouraging people to take the initiative in helping themselves. Crucially, support is only given to women (experience has shown that men cannot be trusted not to gamble and drink the money away), and so while all members of communities benefit from the aid, it also helps to equalize the status of women within the Developing World.

You can make a donation by visiting:
www.mishasomerville.com/bamakoboomboom

## Acknowledgments

This book was written at my folks house in Abriachan, by Loch Ness over the winter of 07/08 when I was ill and unable to do much else. Perhaps because I've hardly written a thing in ten years, this short book took considerable time and effort, and I must thank those that helped make it happen. I would especially like to thank my folks - David and Helena Somerville, for their continued love and support when I was far from my best. I also owe particular thanks to Jamie Armstrong, Amy Todman, Nik Powell and Jock Urquhart for their time, effort and guidance when I was out of my depth and Dr. David Mickel and Lynda Carnochan at Mickel Therapy for much needed help getting better. I would also like to thank Somhairle MacDonald for his imagination and drawings, James Gloyn, Mary Somerville, Sam Bishop, Matt Smith, Emma Donnelly, Rebecca Home, Laurianne Giteau, Ewen Lamont, Jasmin Tulloch, Damien Dussut, Anna Petersdotter, Donnie MacDonald and Peter Clausen for their input in various ways. There are of course many other good friends who have contributed - fragments of ideas from conversations that have made their way in here or there - unfortunately there are too many to mention, but to whom I am in no way less grateful - thanks!

## About the Author

Misha Somerville was born and brought up in the Highlands of Scotland. He moved to Glasgow in 1998 and, after a short spell studying Mechanical Engineering, he spent several years playing with the band *Croft No. Five,* of which he was a founding member. They released two critically acclaimed albums and went on to tour throughout Europe and North America. When the band finished performing he worked as a musical instrument maker - producing and selling low whistles. His instruments are now much sought after and played by musicians around the world. He has always maintained an interest in travelling, and is fascinated by the creative ideas which go into forming cultures around the globe; their music, fashion, art, language, writing and politics. *Bamako Boom Boom* is his first book.

www.mishasomerville.com